Praise for *Gho*

"An inspiring journey of a family's tragedies, celebrations, compassion, and love for each other—through the reflective lens of baseball. Kevin Mulhearn's vivid descriptions of schoolyard fights and baseball games, at various levels, call to mind the language and style of my late colleague, Red Smith."

—Alex Yannis, *New York Times* Sportswriter

"As an attorney for sexual abuse survivors, Kevin Mulhearn has been an indefatigable warrior for justice. As an author, Kevin demonstrates the same level of honesty and courage. Kevin has never been afraid to ask tough questions or take on big institutions, and that's what makes his life and work—as well as this unique memoir—compelling."

—Michael O'Keeffe, *New York Daily News*

"The lessons Kevin Mulhearn learned on Brooklyn's sandlots playing for one of New York City's finest baseball clubs served him well in the years that followed. Somehow he managed to turn grief over his twin brother's untimely death into a legal crusade that brought a measure of peace to victims of sexual abuse committed by a beloved coach at one of the city's top prep schools. In *Ghosts of October*, Mulhearn has turned in a powerful memoir of love, family, grief, recovery, and the enduring powers of baseball."

—Thomas Zambito, *The Journal News*

"In *Ghosts of October*, Kevin Mulhearn shares a powerful, gripping, and transcendent personal and professional story. His love for baseball is matched only by his commitment to justice. The passion he brings to his work has helped many survivors of sexual abuse have their voices heard. Perhaps most importantly, by revealing so much of his own personal journey, Kevin powerfully illustrates just how strongly connected we all are by trauma and abuse that is all around us, and that is all too often unseen and unacknowledged. Kevin's story and his work is a testimony to the idea that when we make the choice to fight for the truth and to fight for healing and justice for others, it can make a difference in ways that we often can't predict. His skill at blending his family narrative with his legal battles and overlaying it all with the metaphors and lessons of baseball is nothing short of spectacular."

—Christopher M. Anderson, Executive Director, MaleSurvivor

"The thread that runs through Kevin Mulhearn's life, work, and moving book is passion—for ground-breaking legal battles on behalf of vulnerable kids and wounded adults, as well as for the game of baseball, a pastime that gives him an anchor through (and sorely-needed break from) these intense professional struggles. This is an inspiring story from a bold and unflinching man whose creative and relentless advocacy for those who've been deeply betrayed will leave you outraged yet hopeful."

—David G. Clohessy, Director, SNAP
(Survivors Network of those Abused by Priests)

"As you begin to read this remarkable book, the first question that pops into your mind is how can this author possibly find commonality between baseball and child sexual abuse? In the hands of most writers it would be an impossible, even unthinkable task but Kevin Mulhearn has pulled it off—and he has done so seamlessly. Kevin is a compassionate and tireless advocate for victims of childhood sexual abuse. While it is a popular news topic, rarely does the public get a clear and thoughtful analysis of the problems faced by victims when they undertake suing those responsible for their victimization. Kevin subtly but forcefully opens a critical and important window into this vexatious problem by weaving in his encyclopedic knowledge and downright love of baseball. His sincerity and thoughtfulness leap off the pages."

—Paul Mones, Esq., Children's Rights Attorney

"Survivors of childhood sexual abuse carry a life-long burden that forever casts a shadow over their lives. When people and institutions that should be dedicated to educating and protecting youngsters fail in their responsibilities, it is up to determined men like Kevin Mulhearn to do something about it. In this book, Kevin speaks eloquently about the terrible plight of those he describes as 'lost boys' and about the need to get justice for the unspeakable crimes against them. I am proud he is also working diligently with me and others to help change the law in New York State so that abusers and those who hide them are held accountable."

—Hon. Margaret A. Markey, New York State Assemblywoman

GHOSTS OF OCTOBER

REFLECTIONS ON LIFE, DEATH AND BASEBALL

Kevin Thomas Mulhearn

NEW YORK

Hard Nock Press, LLC
60 Dutch Hill Rd., Suite 15
Orangeburg, NY 10962
www.HardNockPress.com

Ghosts of October: Reflections on Life, Death and Baseball
Kevin Thomas Mulhearn
First Edition
ISBN 978-0692611371

For my son, Dennis Luke Mulhearn, my pride and joy,

and the keeper of the flame.

-and-

In loving memory of my twin brother, Dennis John Mulhearn, my father, Thomas Lee Mulhearn, and my grandfather, Thomas Joseph Mulhearn. Each of these men—in his inimitable style—taught me to never forget or undervalue the redemptive power of love.

CONTENTS

Part One:

October Skies

Some would have Spring within the heart,
But I, some mellow month in mine
Like old October: flowers depart,
And even youth must resign—
But always, brothers, there are some
To whom no Winters ever come:
Always October skies are theirs,
Even amid life's wintry cares.

—Douglas Malloch, "Make Me Mellow"

Introduction

You have two choices in life. You can dissolve into the main stream, or you can choose to become an achiever and be distinct. To be distinct, you must be different. To be different, you must strive to be what no one else but you can be.

—Alan Ashley-Pitt

D ust to dust.

This ubiquitous three-word sentence purports to sum it all up. We all start as dust and return to dust when we take our last breaths. As proclaimed often in poetry and song, we are nothing more than "dust in the wind."

But I categorically reject that premise. The distance between the first "dust" and the second, as to both time and meaning, must be far greater than can be captured adequately by a two-letter preposition. The long and arduous journey from life to death must count for more than just the metaphysical creation and destruction of our bodies. At the end of the day, when the light flickers for the last time, we must be more than a finely powdered substance reduced by disintegration and decay into the air.

Which leads us to two broad questions: Where do our souls, if such ethereal objects actually exist, play into this dust equation? And what the hell does any of this have to do with baseball?

Patience, friends and foes alike. The answers to both of those questions will unfold as you turn the pages of this book.

CHAPTER ONE

Dust

[T]he ultimate choice for a man, inasmuch as he is driven to transcend himself, is to create or to destroy, to love or to hate.

—Erich Fromm, *The Sane Society*

Our knowledge that we will eventually die is what separates us from the rest of the snorting, sniffing, and scratching animals that inhabit this planet. Our understanding, unique to our species, that life is finite, that we all have an expiration date, compels many a human being to search for some kind of transcendence. [1]

So we need to be vigilant and seize those rare moments when a shimmering jewel peeks out from beneath a pile of mud, begging to be pocketed, and at least gives us a chance to rise above the din of the herd and stake a claim for greatness, for immortality, and for love. Finding love, that often elusive ideal, is the key to unlocking the door to the highest, best, and most noble and everlasting parts of each of us.

The quest for transcendence, as Erich Fromm, a renowned and controversial 20th Century psychologist, accurately noted, also has a dark side. Many a psychopath has deluded himself into thinking that his acts of terror, mass murder, and destruction have served a higher, better, and most noble purpose and, when his body dies, will elevate his spirit to the pantheon. Most of us think that he has doomed himself to the fire and brimstone of hell, but he doesn't give a damn about what most people think; he thinks that he's about to party like a rock star for all eternity with Cleopatra, Marilyn Monroe, a bevy of Hollywood starlets, or seventy-two black-eyed virgins.

It is a bitter irony, therefore, that acts of love and acts of hate often have a common denominator: the actor, whether Good Samaritan or evildoer, perceives his conduct, his dramatic acts, as a bridge to transcendence. That's a wild card that we all just have to live with. But, unfortunately, and too often tragically, sometimes that wild card destroys a really good hand.

We have no way of predicting accurately when the pivotal moments of our lives will occur. There is rarely a clarion call that heralds an upcoming sea change. For good or bad. Nor is there a guide or manual that tells us how to act righteously or for a righteous cause. Or promises that good conduct, smart choices, kindness, compassion, and empathy, will lead inexorably to positive and happy outcomes. Life just doesn't work that neatly. Quite to the contrary, as the old maxim provides, there is only one surefire way to prove that God has a sense of humor: make a plan.

But our inability to predict or control the future is no excuse for wilting in the face of unexpected challenges or changes, no matter how great or awful. We need to be prepared for just about anything. This is the only way to be fully human; a man or woman must be ready to adapt, to change his or her entire life at the strike of a bolt of lightning or the snap of a finger of fate.

Of course this is often not easy. But nothing that comes easy is worth a damn. The struggle has a lot more value than the attained objective. The fight itself, scratching and clawing in the arena while spilling blood, sweat, and tears, matters far more than the decision.

On the morning of September 11, 2001, I was driving to the Westchester County Court in White Plains, New York for a 9:30 a.m. calendar call on a routine criminal matter. I had already negotiated a plea with the Assistant District Attorney. My client, charged with removing hazardous materials from a clean-up site without the proper license, would plead to a misdemeanor and pay a modest fine. We just needed to place the plea deal on the record in open court for the judge to rubber-stamp. It was in all ways a stress-free appearance. My client was eager to get the matter behind her.

I was listening to 620 AM radio, an upstart all-sports station, with the typical over-amped hosts trying to make a name for themselves by pushing the envelope as to good taste and decency. This station's most redeeming quality was that it avoided hard news at all costs. In the morning, I have no tolerance for the talking heads who dissect the news and political scene for the benefit of their captive audiences. I want my radio chatter to be mindless and puerile. For a good while on this beautiful Tuesday morning I was in my element, chilling to sports babble about nothing of consequence.

Then the hosts ruined my tranquility by solemnly reporting that a plane had flown into the North Tower of the World Trade Center. My immediate reaction was to call my brother Sean, who lived in downtown Manhattan and frequently conducted business in or near the World Trade Center. (As a child, I always referred to this complex as the Twin Towers). I was unable to get a signal on my cell phone on the first try, so I kept trying to get through . . . but to no avail.

By the time I had arrived inside the courtroom, the rigid hierarchy of the criminal justice system had—for the day—disappeared. Lawyers, defendants, court officers, and court personnel alike were scurrying about and passing tidbits of information about the incident to each other. Someone said it was a small single-engine plane which had accidentally flown off course. I took a small breath of relief. This could be worse. Unfortunately, of course, it was.

The judge was late to arrive on the bench. She was watching the news on a television inside her chambers. The court clerk served as town crier every few minutes. First he came out to announce that another plane had crashed into the South Tower. At this point we all shuddered as the accident theory had been shattered. I continued to try to reach Sean on the cell. No luck. The busy signal made me want to throw my useless cell phone against the wall. Next report: a plane flew into the Pentagon building in Northern Virginia. We were under attack for sure. How many other planes were in the skies about to hurtle into civilian targets in America's cities? How many were headed for New York and its surrounding areas?

I worried about my kid brother, Thomas, who worked as an architect in Washington, D.C. His office was in Georgetown, miles away from the Pentagon, but he was in a city that was an obvious target for further attacks. I tried to reach Thomas on the cell. Busy. Sean again. Still busy. My imagination started to play nasty tricks on me.

The clerk came out twice more: first to inform us that the South Tower had collapsed, then, minutes later, to report that the North Tower had met the same fate. A woman sitting near me started to cry. "How many people just died?" she wailed. The rest of the people in the courtroom sat in stunned silence. The judge made her way to the bench and sat down gingerly. Her bloodshot eyes were moist.

"My daughter is a senior at Stuyvesant," she said, referring to the elite public high school located a few blocks away from the World Trade Center, "and I haven't been able to reach her." The judge adjourned all matters for the day and told us that the Court would contact us to reschedule all necessary proceedings.

My client looked at me after the judge left the bench and said, "does this mean I have to come back?"

"Yes," I replied, "you have to come back."

On the way back from White Plains to my office in Orangeburg I had to cross the Tappan Zee Bridge, which I had done dozens of times.

On this day, though, I feared that a plane would drop from the sky and take out the bridge with a kamikaze attack. I strained my neck to look for any planes and noticed that several of my fellow bridge-crossers were doing exactly the same thing.

After I crossed the bridge safely I began to again try to get through to Sean and Thomas. Still no luck. I cursed loudly. I drove back alone except for my own thoughts, as I did not dare to turn the radio on again. I did not want to hear any more tragic news. I needed to hear the voices of my brothers. I needed to know that my family was all right.

I arrived back at my office a few minutes before noon, gave my secretary, Deanna, Sean's and Thomas's phone numbers and told her to keep trying to reach those numbers until she got through. A few minutes later my phone rang. It was Thomas.

"You OK?" he asked.

"Yea," I replied. "I only go into the Twin Towers about twice a year for Court of Claims cases. But I'm worried about Sean; I've been trying to get through to him for a couple of hours."

"Sean's fine, Kevin," said Thomas. "I just spoke to him about two minutes ago. He just got out of bed."

"That lazy bastard," I said, with my voice cracking. "Thank God he's so fucking lazy."

Thomas and I both laughed with relief. He told me that he had talked to my mom, dad, and sister, Deirdre, and that everyone was fine. Sean, it turned out, had an appointment in the South Tower of the World Trade Center the next day, September 12th. He missed by but one fateful day from being in the building when the second plane hit. The Mulhearn family, as it was, was still intact.

I went home that day like most Americans and watched the horror unfold on television. It was like a gruesome car wreck from which you could not turn away, only a thousand times worse. Stories about the hospital employees waiting for the injured to stream into their facilities struck a raw nerve. There were few injuries here; the volatile mix of fuel and steel and brick and fire and deluded murderers made sure of that. The smell of death and hate seemed to creep from the airwaves right into my apartment. The body count estimates began to be published and I had no doubt that I would know a number of people who had been killed in the World Trade Center in the most horrific ways imaginable.

Major League Baseball cancelled all ballgames for a few days. When they resumed play in New York, on September 21, 2001, the Mets hosted the Atlanta Braves. All the Mets' players and coaches donned caps that honored New York's service providers. It was strange to see the NYPD and FDNY hats on Major League players; they resembled a softball crew loose in Central Park. All that was missing was a keg in the on-deck circle. Yet when Mike Piazza won the game with a thunderous home run in the bottom of the eighth, the Shea Stadium crowd roared as if the Mets had just clinched the World Series. The crowd, subdued for much of the evening, unleashed a primal scream for the world to hear. We are New York. We celebrate life. We will not be silenced.

For a week or so that mid-September, every day brought news of another boyhood friend who had perished in the Twin Towers. The nuances were unpleasant, to put it mildly, and, as New York's mayor aptly stated, too much to bear. I deliberately avoided hearing any details about how all of these souls met their maker. It was much easier to focus instead on the potential of the Yankees winning their fourth World Series in a row.

I figured that, in the age of parity, if the Yankees could pull it off they would be regarded as the greatest dynasty in the history of baseball. Four in a row and five out of six in the 90s and noughts was a greater feat than even the five consecutive championships of the Yankees—led by Casey Stengel—from 1949 to 1953. For a team to win four consecutive World Championships with the three-tiered playoff system, it had to win twelve consecutive playoff series against the best teams in baseball. Twelve series as opposed to five. The 2001 New York Yankees were on the precipice of immortality.

But when September 2001 died a well-deserved death, the Bronx Bombers seemed destined to follow suit, as they lost the first two games in the best of five American League Division Series against the Oakland A's. When they returned to Yankee Stadium in Game Three, the Yanks nursed a 1-0 lead behind Mike Mussina's gem going into the top of the eighth inning. With two outs and Jeremy Giambi on first base, Terrence Long lined a double down the right field line. Shane Spencer, the right fielder, stumbled in his haste to retrieve the ball and prevent the A's from scoring the tying run. He then heaved an awful throw, well over the head of the cut-off man. His balloon bounced harmlessly to the right of the first base chalk line, when out of nowhere, Derek Jeter, the Yankees' shortstop, grabbed the ball with his bare hand and with a backhanded flip redirected it to home plate. Jorge Posada, the catcher, and Giambi, the baserunner, both seemed startled that there was going to be a play at the plate. Posada fielded the ball and made a quick swipe tag on Jeremy Giambi's upper right calf. The play was bang-bang, and the umpire, perhaps not giving the runner the benefit of the doubt because he failed to slide (thus breaking a cardinal rule of baseball), punched Giambi out with an emphatic signal.

It was a remarkable play, not for any tremendous athletic prowess, but for the uncanny headiness of Jeter to be in the right place at the right time. These Yankees did not lose easily.

After taking care of business in Game Four, the Yanks returned to Oakland on October 15th for the fifth and deciding game. The only problem for my family was that on this night my sister, Deirdre, went into labor in Freehold Hospital in Freehold, New Jersey.

After she became pregnant, Deirdre had decided to break up with Michael, her French-Canadian fiancee. She was far from alone, though, as my mother, father, brother Sean, and I, all made our way to Freehold Hospital, which we remembered all too well from my twin brother Dennis's numerous visits to the hospital's psychiatric ward in the early

1990s. Now, fortunately, this hospital held the promise of life rather than disease and heart-break.

The medical staff had made a mistake in waiting too long to give Deirdre an epidural injection in her back to ease her labor pains. She had dilated too much, too quickly, and was on her own. I entered the maternity room while Deirdre and my mother were complaining about the staff's failure to give her an epidural in time. I told Deirdre that it was no big deal and that she just had to "suck it up." She cursed at me like a drunken sailor and demanded that I leave the room.

Eager for a Yankees update, I was glad to oblige. I wandered the hospital until I found a waiting area with a television. Roger Clemens pushed off the mound and threw a fastball by an A's batter. I scrambled to find my father and brother; Deirdre had several hours to go before she gave birth.

My mother was with Deirdre and my sister was deprived of any painkillers. The waiting room was a wonderful place for the Mulhearn men to convene in solidarity. In time, Deirdre gave birth to a son, Christian Thomas Michael Mulhearn, who was blessed to be born on a playoff series clinching evening. He was an honorary Yankees fan before he had his first taste of mother's milk.

Deirdre apologized for snapping at me. I did not mind. I looked at the beautiful face of her child, the first Mulhearn born in more than a quarter of a century, and imagined him in pinstripes.

The Yankees made short work of the Seattle Mariners in the American League Championship Series. The Mariners had won an astonishing one hundred and sixteen games in the regular season, only to fall meekly to the Yanks in five games. The Yankees had the look of a steamroller destined to flatten anyone who dared try to erase their mark of greatness.

The scene shifted to Arizona where the Yankees were to begin the World Series against the upstart Arizona Diamondbacks, who were led by two outstanding pitchers: Randy Johnson and Curt Schilling. I watched every pre-game show on television and read all the newspaper stories about the Series with manic intensity. As long as I could focus on baseball and the great Yankees of 2001 I was able to block out the horrific thoughts of 9/11 and the carnage wreaked upon my city by the mad, ruthless murderers.

In Game Seven, which I watched alone in my Blauvelt, New York apartment, the Yankees were just an inning away from claiming another world title. I realized, though, even before the final inning unfolded, that during that cold, dark autumn of 2001 I had immersed myself into the success of the Yankees as a prophylactic and artificial balm against the imposing backdrop of the horrors of 9/11.

I was luckier than many that day, as I had not lost any relatives or close friends. But in the weeks that followed, as the names of the dead were made public, I was shocked that so many of my childhood friends, classmates, and acquaintances—an even dozen—had perished in the rubble of the Twin Towers.

In my memory, at least, these men never escaped their Brooklyn adolescences. When I pictured them in the steel-framed buildings before they plunged to the earth, I could see only the faces of boys who still maintained the care-free exuberance of youth and refused to accept any limitations, self-imposed or otherwise, as to the breadth of their accomplishments and capacity for joy. This myopic, one-dimensional, and distorted view of the victims only made their passing seem all the more tragic and senseless.

I pictured several of them on the sandlots of Brooklyn: Marine Park, Seaview Park, the Parade Grounds, Shore Road—the places where I learned how to be a man, where I learned that failure, although inevitable, must always be viewed as a temporary condition, lest it turn into an immovable monolith, where success was always right around the corner, where one good swing can erase long phases of futility and frustration. They learned, no doubt, the same lessons, but now . . .

The Yankees were going to uplift me and the entire City of New York through the pain of 9/11. Their victory would stand as a testament to the human spirit, to the resilience of New Yorkers, and as a monument to the memory of the victims.

On the mound was Mariano Rivera, the incomparable relief pitcher. The best that ever was, even the old men had to admit. The Yankees' one run lead might as well as have been ten. After Mariano mowed down the Diamondbacks in the bottom of the eighth, I made my victory calls to my father and brothers. Not so fast, they cautioned, the game isn't over yet. Nonsense, I replied, don't you see who's pitching for us.

Leading off in the bottom of the ninth Mark Grace shoots a flare past the second baseman. No problem, just a lone baserunner. The next batter, Damian Miller, the Diamondbacks' catcher, bunts right back to Rivera—the best athlete on the field, mind you—and he whirls and throws to Derek Jeter at short. The ball tails at the last second, and Jeter, playing with an injured leg, is unable to corral the throw. Now I'm worried.

Several batters later, Rivera makes a great pitch to Luis Gonzalez, and jams him badly, but Gonzalez is strong enough to bloop the ball over the drawn-in Jeter to just beyond his normal shortstop depth. Jay Bell, who reached base on a failed sacrifice bunt attempt, runs in from third base, arms raised in triumph, and jumps on the plate. Mariano Rivera, the unparalleled relief pitcher who has blown the game, and the Series, walks off the field with his head held high, but with pain and disappointment etched on his face.

I turn off the television the moment the winning run crosses home plate and jump into bed without bothering to wash my face or brush my teeth. I close my eyes and am struck, like a punch to the gut, by a tidal wave of emotion. Gleaming through the darkness, my visions are clear, colorful, and stark.

I see Jay Burnside, my affable, easy-going Cadets teammate, snapping off a nasty curveball. I see Danny Suhr, Kings Bay mainstay, grinning through his catcher's mask, trash-talking as I dig my spikes into the batter's box. I see Chris "Shady" Grady, who played for both the Cadets and the Poly Prep Blue Devils, patrolling right field with one eye fixed on the game and the other on all the pretty girls who are walking past him. I see Joe Mascali, older brother of Poly Prep teammate, Arnie, making sure that my tables at the Royale—a wedding banquet hall for Orthodox Jews on McDonald and Ditmas (in which Dennis, Sean and I had worked as waiters)—were clean as a whistle. I see Paul Martini, St. Thomas Aquinas classmate and comedian, trying to fend off the vicious blows of our teacher after Paul had unwittingly stepped on an open wound—no doubt evoking a childhood torment—by jokingly calling him "Brother Donald Duck."

All gone now. Brought down well before their time by the evil whims of madmen. Those bastards. Dust to dust.

And I see my twin brother, Dennis, who died two years shy of thirty, way before *his* time. I see him across from me, glove in hand, firing a baseball in my direction. Thousands of throws, each a reminder of how lucky I am to have Dennis as my best friend and constant companion. I think again of 9/11 and for a moment am thankful that Dennis—as gentle a soul as one could ever find—was not alive to see the carnage of that awful day. I don't think he could have handled the colossal unfairness of it all.

I weep silently that night; the tears flow freely for my brother, for those unfortunate souls who were in the wrong place at the wrong time on 9/11, for their family members whose grief and suffering will no doubt be unimaginable, and for the savagery of mankind. That night the Yankees, and especially their great relief pitcher, are not able to shield me from the sorrow.

But in retrospect it was too much to ask for anyway. Baseball is just a game. 9/11 was real life, shorn of humanity, its cruelest manifestation. I'm pretty sure that I would have felt much the same way that night even if the Yankees had won. The game, the Series, were just distractions . . .

simple, petty, juvenile distractions from the ugly reality that the world had changed. And not for the better.

Alone in my apartment, no longer able to ignore the flood of grotesque images, I am unable to sleep. My very soul has been stirred and it will not easily be settled. The outcome of the 2001 World Series is already just a distant blip on my radar. In just a few short minutes the protective screen of baseball has crashed to the ground and shattered into millions of tiny pieces.

I think of the terror and panic that my long-ago friends must have felt as thousands of tons of free-falling steel and iron and concrete descended upon them. I see the horror in their faces as they realized that the unspeakable, the unimaginable, was actually happening. And then I can think of only one thing.

Dust . . .

CHAPTER TWO

Poppy

In matters of truth and justice, there is no difference between large and small problems, for issues concerning the treatment of people are all the same.

—Albert Einstein

Thomas Joseph Mulhearn, my paternal grandfather, was the smartest man I ever knew, yet he never even graduated from high school. Legend has it that he was the top-rated student at Erasmus Hall High School in Brooklyn (back in the old days when Erasmus was an elite school) but had to drop out in his junior year to help support his family. The first Mulhearn family trade, as taught by Patrick "Gaffer" Mulhearn, my first-generation Irish-American ancestor, was bricklaying. Many of the early twentieth century churches in Brooklyn were built by construction crews supervised by my great-grandfather, who was renowned more for his prodigious strength and hollow leg than his piety.

On one such project, my grandfather, then in his early twenties, fell off a two-story building. Although he survived to tell the tale, he was left with a severely damaged right hip, and foreclosed from ever stepping up the ladder to join the second family business: the New York City Police Department, in which all three of his younger brothers flourished.

My father, Thomas Lee (my grandmother's maiden name) Mulhearn, was an only child, but he and my mother (born Mary Ann Montello) gave my grandfather five grandchildren: me, Dennis, Sean, Deirdre, and Thomas. Born on October 20, 1964, I was the oldest, having kicked out of my mother's womb seven minutes earlier than my twin, Dennis. Sean was born in August 1966; Deirdre was born in December 1969, two months after the Miracle Mets shocked the world; and Thomas was born on September 11, 1974.

My grandfather almost always radiated joy when he was in our presence. It was simultaneously comforting and yet daunting to realize that we were the world to him. I could not bear to disappoint my grandfather, even more than my own parents, because even as a child it was obvious that Poppy's hopes rested on us, rather than himself.

In early 1975, after my grandmother died suddenly of a stroke while just in her mid-fifties, Poppy moved into our basement in our row-home on Kimball Street between Avenue P and Quentin Road. Our basement had three separate but conjoined rooms after the stairwell: the outside laundry room, the middle room which was Poppy's bedroom, and the far inside room which Dennis and I shared. When my mother went back to work as a kindergarten teacher in a local Catholic school, my grandfather assumed the primary role of taking care of my baby brother Thomas. Thanks to Poppy's rapt attention and expert tutelage, Thomas was reading by the time he was three.

My siblings and I were lucky enough to get to know my grandfather quite well. Poppy was a quiet and introspective man who used words sparingly. He prided himself above all else on his honesty and integrity. My grandfather's word was worth more than a mere handshake. He promised only what he could deliver and usually delivered more than he promised.

In my youth, I cannot remember Poppy ever leaving the borough of Brooklyn. When my family visited relatives in Staten Island or New Jersey, Poppy would insist on staying home and immersed himself in crossword puzzles, which he finished with remarkable speed and precision. When my father invited friends over to our house, Poppy would usually exchange pleasantries and then burrow himself into the basement. As far as I know, my grandfather loved only two things in life: his family and baseball. What his passions lacked in quantity, however, were more than compensated for by the depth of his devotion.

I remember waiting for him to come home from work as a machinist at American Machine & Foundry. We could see him from far down the block as his uneven gait was unmistakable. My father told me that my grandfather never missed a day of work in thirty years. No such thing as a sick day for Thomas Joseph Mulhearn. He would see us running toward him, break into a broad smile and take out some treats—often a handful of Reese's Peanut Butter Cups—from his pocket.

Once, when Dennis and I were about twelve, we told my grandfather that we could not get good reception on our small black and white television. When we returned home from school, Poppy had made six detailed drawings worthy of a graphic artist which illustrated the different positions of the antennae required to obtain a clear picture for each channel.

Poppy died after a heart attack on October 27, 1978. During the three years he lived with us, he had numerous opportunities, in the grand tradition of the Irish raconteur, to fill our heads with stories. Since Dennis and I were only fourteen-years-old when Poppy died, I don't remember too many stories about politics, history, women. Those may have been intended to come later, or maybe not. I do recall a bunch of tales about his brothers and sister but mostly I remember Poppy talking about baseball.

He loved everything about the game. My grandfather played ball before Little League, uniforms, or umpires. If they did not have enough kids to form a full squad they would play a version of baseball with only two or three bases. He was a pitcher and a first baseman, and a southpaw. I can still recall the look of pride on his face when he told us, with just a hint of braggadocio, about several no-hitters that he had pitched in big games.

In his mid-twenties, my grandfather took a turn at coaching a group of twelve-year-olds in a competitive sandlot league. He almost created a mutiny when he put his three best fielders in the outfield. Poppy explained his thinking to us: if an infielder made an error it would only cost one base, but if an outfielder let a ball get past him on the open sandlot fields he would give the other team three or four bases. After some initial resistance (the good fielders all wanted to play short or third), Poppy's team rounded into form and steamrolled through the regular season without a loss. On playoff Saturday, however, they played a doubleheader with a game in the morning and the championship game in the late afternoon. His team won the first game handily and had two or three hours to wait for the final game. It was a hot and humid day, so Poppy instructed his team to sit under some trees and relax. They refused to listen, though, and ran around like wild men until game time. According to Poppy, the heat had exhausted them so they played the afternoon game like zombies and lost to a team they had trounced in the regular season. Poppy could not abide his team's disobedience and disrespect and he quit on the spot, never to coach again, not even after my father began to demonstrate some real talent for baseball.

I figure that season to have taken place in 1934 or 1935. The members of my grandfather's team of twelve-year-olds, if still alive, are about ninety-three-years-old. I would pay good money to talk to someone who played on that team. What does he remember about Poppy? What does he remember about the championship game?

Some of those twelve-year-old kids probably served our nation in World War II. It is remarkable to me that a game that was played by children more than seventy years ago still sticks in my conscience. It means something to me because it meant something to my grandfather. Baseball, as is so often the case, links me to the dead.

When Dennis, I, and Sean started to play baseball, we were startled by the Jekyll and Hyde transformation of Poppy. As a rule, my grandfather conducted himself with considerable restraint and dignity. He was usually polite to a fault and rarely complained about anything. When he died of a heart attack, my grandfather's autopsy revealed that he had previously suffered significant heart damage. He never saw a doctor, although upon his death we found dozens of Tums and Rolaids packets in his room. In all likelihood Poppy had suffered silently through several mild heart attacks without saying a word about it to anyone. His unique self-prescription for coronary disease, apparently, was the ingestion of antacids.

At our baseball games, however, it was a different story. My grandfather was a one man holy terror and waged a constant verbal war on the umpires. He never used profanity but he loudly and incessantly questioned the eyesight and integrity of the men in blue. They were always trying to cheat his grandkids. It was an unpleasant sideshow to our games and I remember cowering in embarrassment, praying silently that my beloved grandfather would just shut up and let us play in peace. He never could keep silent, though.

I now see what I could not fathom as a child. My grandfather's life was a series of disappointments from beginning to end: dropping out of high school, injuring his hip, losing his beloved wife far earlier than he had wanted. He knew that he had not even begun to tap his potential; he lived a simple, parochial life because, for his time and in his circumstances, no other life was available to him. Yet his pride and dignity did not permit him to ever voice any disappointment or anger at the hand he was dealt.

But the mask of the stoic was not a perfect fit. At the ballfields, Poppy had a forum in which to unleash his pent-up frustration. By transferring his rage to the umpires, on matters which concerned him only indirectly, he could rationalize his behavior and not—in his own mind—deviate from his personal code which mandated that he swallow his grievances. The theme was constant: DO NOT CHEAT MY GRANDSONS. DO NOT CHEAT MY GRANDSONS. The rants, the aberrant behavior, were my grandfather's way of tacitly informing all who would listen that although he was cheated with respect to his own life, he would not permit his grandchildren to likewise be cheated. For all his intelligence, I wonder if Poppy ever realized that that was the reason he was so relentless in his verbal assaults against our umpires.

Poppy's anger at crooked umpires was not always misplaced. During a C.Y.O. Baseball tournament, when we were about eleven, Dennis and I played for our local parish, St. Thomas Aquinas, against several other Brooklyn parish teams. We won the first game 1-0. Dennis and I both pitched several scoreless innings and I drove in the lone run of the game. The championship game was a laugher as we exploded for a 12-1 victory. Dennis and I again pitched a number of scoreless innings and I had two extra base hits and drove in three or four runs. After our victory celebration, as we waited for the awards presentation, I expected to win the large tournament MVP trophy. It was not to be. The MVP winner, chosen by the home plate umpire, was none other than the pitcher on the team we had just bombed, who, coincidentally, was driven to the game by his neighbor, the home plate umpire. Well, Poppy, who was then in his early sixties, went into a wild fury, with veins popping and arms flailing, he started limping toward the umpire with every intention of popping him. My Uncle Harry, Poppy's younger brother (and a former captain in the New York City Police Department, who literally wrote the book on police procedure), had to grab Poppy and drag him, screaming and sputtering, to his car.

"It's not right. It's not right. You can't do that to a kid. It's not right. You can't cheat my grandson like that. It's not right."

His words still resonate. The world is often unfair. People are often unfair. But don't accept an injustice without a fight. I never saw my grandfather in such a rage. Of course, in the grand scheme of things an MVP trophy is not the be-all and end-all. But it wasn't the trophy that he fought for that day, it was the principle. Right is right. Wrong is wrong. You can't blur the difference. And, when you see a wrong, you owe it to yourself and others to do everything in your power to right that wrong.

When he had calmed down that day, Poppy was still so upset that he was almost on the verge of tears. The injustice of the umpire's decision rankled him to the bone. His goal in life was to make sure that his grandchildren wanted for nothing, AND WERE NOT CHEATED.

What Poppy realized on that day, and what wounded him so, was the realization that despite his best efforts he could not always protect us from being cheated.

No man is bulletproof, Poppy.

I am grateful that my grandfather was not alive to see what happened to Dennis.

CHAPTER THREE

Wiff

Satisfaction lies in the effort, not in the attainment, full effort is full victory.

—Mahatma Gandhi

My father continued the family tradition as a member of the New York City Police Department, although I am fairly certain that none of his predecessors ever quite had his knack of playing all the angles and looking for the proverbial score at every opportunity. By the time Dennis and I were seven or so, my father spent a good deal of his time as a New York City cop plotting his sons' baseball futures.

I remember well the first day that we actually played baseball, not some powder-puff facsimile with a rubber ball or wiffle bat, but baseball. Horsehide leather with red stitches and a wooden baseball bat. The ball was easily obtainable at any sporting goods store, but the bat for two skinny seven-year-olds required a little more imagination.

My father, who could not fairly be described as handy, had purchased a regulation thirty-two inch baseball bat with a thin handle. He then sawed the top end of the bat off about halfway down the barrel, sawed off a two inch cap from the very top of the bat, and crazy glued the home-made cap on top of the shortened handle portion. He had made a mini-regulation baseball bat. The aesthetics of the bat suffered a bit from the gray electrical tape wrapped around the makeshift cap as an insurance policy for the crazy glue, but my father nonetheless presented the bat to us with justifiable pride. Dennis and I looked at each other. This was not just playtime anymore. This was a solemn occasion.

We drove from our house on Kimball Street to the Avenue S and East 32nd Street parking lot for Marine Park, a sprawling park with about a dozen baseball fields of divergent quality. The fields weren't much to look at but they were still baseball fields. The sunken mounds, uneven grass, batter's box trenches, etc., did not diminish these fields in our young eyes. As soon as we parked, we started running from the car toward the nearest field, but my father yelled at us to stop.

"Slow down boys, we're playing over there."

He pointed to a patch of grass behind the tennis courts. A black iron fence about two feet high circled the area. This was the birthplace of our baseball careers. We hopped the fence and my father walked to the corner of the grassy area and gently placed the bat, standing up from the barrel side, against the fence. For about half an hour we threw the ball to each other. Then my father dropped out of the game and it was just me and Dennis. Neither of us had a particularly good arm but we each loved to throw and catch. We could do it for hours . . . and the simple joy of the throw and the catch would not diminish as the years passed.

When my father was satisfied that we had mastered the rudiments of throwing and catching, he finally turned toward the bat. "Who wants to hit?"

We both ran for the bat and I grabbed it a split second before Dennis could. He lowered his head and looked crestfallen. "It's all right Dennis, you'll get your turn soon enough. I'll give you each twenty swings," said my dad.

My father was a hitting technician without peer in Brooklyn, and had drilled in us the fine points of a good baseball stance: knuckles aligned properly, hands at shoulder height and slightly away from the body, feet even with the shoulders, knees slightly bent. The swing instructions were also consistent: wait, wait , wait . . . step . . . level swing, attack the baseball. And, above all things, hit it where it was pitched. Outside pitches needed to be hit to right, down the middle to center, and inside to left. These core principles never changed in the nearly ten years that my father coached us.

From the start, I was a decent hitter. My father threw overhand about twenty feet away from me and I hit more pitches than I missed. A few grounders, some weak pop ups, and some line drives, a few of which even cleared the fences.

"Attaboy," my dad barked after one of my good hits—he always liked to end a hitting session on a positive note. "Give your brother a shot."

Dennis grabbed the bat but to his considerable chagrin did not match my success with the wooden bat. He kept missing pitch after pitch. Nothing but air for a long while. At first I reveled in his failure, but after a few minutes of quietly celebrating my brother's futility my air of superiority gave way to genuine empathy. My father began to tinker with Dennis's swing in an effort to improve the results. Move your elbow there. Start your hands out here. Open your feet a little more. Widen your stance. Keep your eyes on the ball. Just meet the ball . . . don't try to kill it.

Nothing worked. Dennis could not make any contact with the baseball. My father began to get exasperated. His face and neck turned purple and his constructive suggestions gave way to blunt commands.

"C'mon. Hit the damn ball. For God's sake, this is not that hard."

Dennis was almost turning blue from the effort of trying to hit a baseball. No man or boy who ever struck out ever tried to make contact harder than Dennis did that day. Dennis was fighting back tears due to his futility and my father's growing impatience. But even as a seven-year-old Dennis was a tough kid. He did not cry and most importantly he did not quit.

My father's exhortations had ended. He threw the ball in stone cold silence. Wiff. Wiff. Wiff. C'mon, Dennis, I said to myself. Hit the baseball. Hit the ball. Wiff. Five minutes more of stance tinkering and swing instructions. Wiff. Wiff. Wiff. Silence . . . worse than an obscenity.

My father rested his glove hand on his hip and looked in toward the batter. He finally settled on a radical overhaul, borne of frustration and desperation.

"Dennis, let's try something different. Take the bat and get on the other side of the plate."

Dennis complied and stood in the makeshift left-handed batter's box. Same principles but backwards. My father tossed the ball and Dennis took his first ever left-handed swing. He hit a sharp grounder right at me. "Way to go, Dennis," I screamed.

My father gave him an Attaboy. Dennis smiled from ear to ear. He took about ten more lefty swings, hit a few, missed a few, until on his final swing, he connected squarely with the baseball and deposited it far over the black metal fence. My father was satisfied.

"That's enough for today, boys. Good job."

We gathered our equipment and headed for the car. Dennis had salvaged his baseball career from his inauspicious start. My father would never have imagined that his desperate swing change for Dennis would in time prove to be a stroke of genius. Dennis and I left Marine Park happy and proud. On this day, finally, we were baseball players.

CHAPTER FOUR

Cadets

Baseball gives a growing boy self-poise and self-reliance. Baseball is a man maker.

—Al Spalding

When I was a young boy my mom used to take my siblings and me to St. Thomas Aquinas Church every Sunday morning. While fidgeting in the pew during Mass, I would usually read the church bulletin which provided weekly reports on parish activities, including scores of St. Thomas's youth sports teams' games. St. Thomas had excellent baseball teams in the early 1970s but every time one of its teams made it to a league championship game it seemed to lose to a team called the Cadets.

When I returned home from church one day, I asked my father about the Cadets.

"The Cadets are the best baseball organization in Brooklyn," my dad said.

"Did you play for them?" I asked.

"No. I played for a team called the Flynn Celtics, and later the Cardinals. But we played the Cadets all the time."

"Who usually won?" I asked. My father's dismissive grunt answered my question.

On a warm day in the Summer of 1973 my dad took me and Dennis for a walk around the cement track at Marine Park. Outside the track and to the right of the Avenue S parking lot was Diamond 13, a short Little League field that faced a residential block, East 33rd Street, just beyond the trees in deep left field. Inside the track were a number of full-scale baseball fields (including Diamonds 6, 7, 8, 9, and 10).

As we were finishing our walk and headed back to my dad's car, we passed a stocky man in his mid-forties with glasses, a buzz-top haircut, and a noticeable limp. He recognized my father and greeted him as if he were his long-lost son. The man introduced himself to us and then pulled my father away for a brief but animated conversation. They shook hands and the man gave Dennis and me a friendly wave before departing.

"Who was that?" Dennis asked our father.

"That was Jim McElroy, the Head of the Cadets. Around here they call him 'Mr. Baseball.'"

My father explained that Jim McElroy was the long-time manager of the Cadets' older baseball teams, had achieved remarkable success, coached a bunch of major leaguers, including Joe Torre, and had even won a national championship one year in Johnstown, Pennsylvania, a town notorious for its historic flood. (James McElroy Jr., now eighty-five, is still the Chairman of the Cadets Baseball Club. He has been affiliated with the Cadets, as a player, coach, manager, chairman and director, since 1944—when he played on the very first Brooklyn Cadets team). [2]

"You're in luck, boys," my father said. "Mr. McElroy has a son about your age and wants me to help him coach a team in the Marine Park League next year." We had no idea at the time of the pleasures that awaited us.

The next year, after our first scrimmage, Jim McElroy threw up his hands and acknowledged that he did not have the patience to coach a bunch of unskilled nine-year-olds. He handed off the managing reins to my father. My dad then embarked on a magnificent eight-year run as a youth baseball manager for the Brooklyn Cadets.

In my dad's first season as manager, we were crushed in our first game by the Rams, a team from Sheepshead Bay. My father made a few adjustments. He converted our biggest and strongest player, Steve Kopchik—who had a rifle arm, from a catcher into a pitcher. We practiced almost every night in the gloaming at Marine Park. By the end of the season, we were winning almost every game, including those against the Rams.

By then my father had the youth baseball bug. He began to recruit some of the best players in Brooklyn and Queens with an eye on fielding a championship team. Our league, the American Amateur Baseball Congress ("AABC"), had city, regional, and national playoffs in late July and early August.

When Dennis and I were eleven, in 1976, my dad recruited Wayne Rosenthal, a tall and strong football player for the Canarsie Rattlers, for our Cadets team. Wayne was a tough kid; he regularly ripped up his knees and thighs sliding on the rocky fields of Marine Park but, regardless of how much of his own blood he spilled, he never came out of any game. He could pitch, catch, or play short, and was an outstanding baserunner and the only kid on our team with both the confidence and bat control to regularly lay down bunt hits with two strikes.

Eventually, after starring at South Shore High School and St. John's University, Wayne pitched in relief for the Texas Rangers for forty-two games in 1991 and 1992. He also was the pitching coach for the Florida Marlins when they beat the Yankees in six games in the 2003 World Series. After the Yankees lost Game Six in 2003, my brother Sean called me and said, "well, at least Wayne got a ring." Minutes later my brother Thomas called me and repeated the same line almost word for word.

When we were twelve, our out-manned Cadets team somehow won the North Atlantic regional tournament in Waterbury, Connecticut. In the first game of the regionals we upset a heavily favored team from

Connecticut, which started a tall, flame-throwing lefty against us. We won a 1-0 nailbiter on a late, long home run to center field by Wayne Rosenthal. We played the rest of the tournament with house money and prevailed in the final over a strong team from Perry Hall, Maryland, behind five home runs over the short outfield fences—a far cry from the cavernous, open sandlot fields of Marine Park.

We were dispatched quickly in the double-elimination World Series in Forest Park, Georgia, but, like a shark after its first smell of blood in the water, we were hungry for more. For the next two years, I, Dennis, and many of our Cadets teammates: Mike Gambino, Dennis Tighe, Kendall Mabry, Wayne Rosenthal, to name just a few, dreamed of returning to the grand stage of the World Series for another shot at sandlot glory. We were all pretty much obsessed about this goal.

That same year, 1977, my father also managed my brother Sean's ten-year-old team and guided that team to the ten-year-old AABC World Series. At the time no other manager in AABC history had taken two different teams, at different age-levels, to the World Series in the same year. Sean's team finished that season with the remarkable record of sixty-five wins against three losses (with two losses in the World Series). That team was probably the best squad that my father ever managed.

By the time Dennis and I were fourteen, in 1979, the Brooklyn Cadets were one of the best teams in the country. That year my father managed just our team; his good friend, Harry Maxwell, a tough, no-nonsense, charismatic, former U.S. Marine and New York City police officer, managed Sean's team.

We played doubleheaders on Saturdays and Sundays and four or five games on weeknights. This exhausting eight or nine games a week schedule sharpened our skills to a fine edge. We steamrolled through the playoffs, won a thriller in the Brooklyn championship game against Gil Hodges—our nemesis from Bay Ridge—and took care of business in the regional tournament in Ridgewood, New Jersey.

In the regional championship game, Dennis Tighe Jr., a tall, skinny, red-headed righthander, who had an excellent curve and outstanding command of his fastball, shut down a solid team from Warwick, New Jersey. After the last out was made and we had secured a ticket to the fourteen-year-old AABC World Series in Knoxville, Tennessee—home of Tim McCarver Stadium—Dennis Tighe pulled out a boom box radio from his bag and cranked up the volume to the Queen song, "We are the Champions."

"No time for losing. Because we are the Champions . . . of the world."

Dennis's father, Dennis Tighe Sr., a New York City cop and one of our coaches, became irate and yelled at Dennis to turn off the damn boom box. The music was turned off but not our confidence. Unlike when we were twelve, when we were just happy to be in the World Series, in the Summer of 1979 we knew we belonged. We believed that we had the skills: the pitching, hitting, and fielding, and the will, to win the national tournament and claim bragging rights as the best team in the United States.

In early August 1979, when our bus pulled into our hotel parking lot in Knoxville after a long and tiring drive, my father turned and addressed our team.

"Fellas, you should be very proud of getting this far. But let's not be content to just be here. Let's give it our best shot and see what happens."

My father then talked to us about scheduling and protocols.

"One last thing. After we eat tonight you guys can walk around and explore a little bit. But curfew is at 10:00 p.m. If you are not in your rooms and in bed by 10:00 p.m., you will not play tomorrow. And don't test me on that."

Ten of the thirteen players on our team were in bed by 10:00 p.m. that night. But three were not: Dennis Tighe, our best pitcher, Dave Bogatz, our center fielder and the hitting star of the regional series—he had clocked several home runs, and Kendall Mabry, our left fielder and one of our best power hitters. These three had not gone far; they had merely walked around the perimeter of the hotel. None of them had been wearing a watch. On the way back to their rooms, this tardy trio bumped into our coaches: my dad, Dennis Tighe Sr., and Pat Lynch—whose son, John, was my best friend (besides my twin) at my high school, Poly Prep—who were on their way to the hotel bar. My father looked at his watch. It was a few minutes after 10:30 p.m.

The next day the players on our team were shocked when we looked at our lineup. Dennis Tighe was not pitching, and he, Dave Bogatz, and Kendall Mabry, were not starting or, as it turned out, playing. We lost a tight game to a team from Michigan with a right-handed pitcher who kept us off balance with a slow curveball.

It must have killed my father, who had worked tirelessly that summer to ensure the success of this team, to bench three of his best players in the most important game of the season, but he could not tolerate their disobedience, irresponsibility, and cavalier breach of his curfew. My father stuck to his guns, honored his word, and suffered the consequences.

The 1979 fourteen-year-old Cadets did not win the AABC national championship. And our subsequent Cadets teams, although talented and hungry, would never be quite good enough to make it to another World Series.

CHAPTER FIVE

Lucky Kid

All who would win joy, must share it; happiness was born a twin.

—Lord Byron

Almost every child who lived on Kimball Street went to St. Thomas Aquinas Elementary School, which was located just a few blocks away on Hendricksen Street and Flatbush Avenue. The most oppressive aspect of this Catholic school was its strict policy of segregating boys and girls. The girls had their own school in a building right across the street, but the distance in emotional terms felt like miles. For most of us, girls were a strange species. Not many of the boys had the stones to engage the girls in banter, or more. Those who could were given considerable respect by the timid masses.

One unintended side effect of this segregation policy was an increase in male aggression. It would be the rare week when a serious fight did not take place on or near school grounds. The fighting ritual repeated itself time and time again like a bizarre scene from *Lord of the Flies*. The two fighters would square off and the horde of onlookers would form a circle, sometimes locking arms, and shout out a chant that included a nasty racial slur.

This slur was not uttered against any specific minority target, as St. Thomas did not have any black students. Nor were there any Hispanic, Asian, or Indian students. St. Thomas was lily white: mostly Irish, but with a liberal sprinkling of Italian, Polish, and various other European ethnicities thrown into the melting pot.

The fighting etiquette was crystal clear: the combatants would engage until one was standing and the other was not. Unless the fight was broken up by a faculty member, there was always a winner and a loser. It was a serious transgression for any student observer to participate in the fight, other than to occasionally throw a beaten party trying to get out of the circle back to his foe for more punishment.

When I was about twelve I took a turn inside the sparring circle. I was an odd kid, always being criticized by my teachers for looking out the window instead of paying attention in class. He's a bright boy, they would tell my mother, but he has to stop all that daydreaming. I couldn't help it, though, for the world beyond the borders of St. Thomas, or for that matter Brooklyn itself, always fascinated me more than the rote curriculum which was being spoon-fed to us in class.

One day I tired of the indignities being inflicted upon me by the bully crowd: stupid things like kids stealing my hat or snapping me with a rubber band. On this particular day I just had had enough of the petty torments and decided to assert myself. I did so by calling out one of the biggest and toughest bullies in the school, James Alutto, for a fight during lunch break. At first he did not believe that I had the audacity to challenge him to a fight.

"You're kidding me, right?"

"No, I'm dead serious. I'll see you in the schoolyard."

The bully turned vicious. "You're dead, motherfucker. You're dead."

My friends tried to convince me to back out of the fight. What are you crazy. He'll kick your ass. You're dumber than you look. Alutto is a bad dude. I stood my ground. It was too late to back out without being pilloried for the balance of my school career. More importantly, I wanted to win, to stand up to the bully, to stand up for myself once and for all.

Alutto showed up in the schoolyard with his posse. He took his shirt off, stood before me in an Italian tuxedo tank-top, ingloriously known in Brooklyn as a "wife-beater," and revealed the type of muscles that I was still years away from acquiring myself. A circle formed and the usual fight chant began.

I started jabbing Alutto with combination punches thrown in a mixed brew of rage and fear. I popped him on the face several times. He swung wildly and I ducked to avoid the blows. I kept jabbing him. My fist crashed into his mouth. And then his nose. Blood started to trickle down his face. My peers stood in disbelief. Mulhearn is kicking Alutto's ass. I moved in for the kill and popped a few more jabs. I was close to my foe . . . too close. Alutto unleashed a vicious overhead right and connected squarely with my forehead. He was wearing a heavy skull and crossbones ring on his middle finger; it dug into my flesh.

I was numb with pain. The fight immediately drained from me. Alutto, embarrassed by his early futility, carved me up with a bunch of precision shots to my unprotected face. I crumbled to the ground holding my bloody nose. I didn't scream, at least, but I could not stop the steady flow of tears. Unwilling to accept victory, Alutto finished me with a few hard kicks to my ribs and then, finally, posse in tow, marched triumphantly from the scene of the battle.

In the end I had suffered a beating like few others inflicted in the St. Thomas schoolyard. As the crowd dispersed, I heard the murmurs. That was something else. What a fight. Little solace. My friend, Tom Buonanno, helped me to my feet. I was too wobbly to walk without assistance. Tom and another friend, Paul Martini, helped me walk the three blocks to my house.

My grandfather was home. He had made sandwiches for me, Dennis, Sean, and Deirdre, and was getting concerned because I was almost twenty minutes late. He saw that I was bleeding from the lip, nose, and forehead, and he turned ghostly white.

"What the heck happened to you?" he asked while immediately administering to my wounds. I relayed the story to the best of my woozy recollection. My grandfather started muttering about getting us out of that school. Too many ruffians. Too dangerous. This is not right.

Dennis, listening intently all the while, could take no more. "James Alutto did this to you?" he asked, his voice quivering in rage. I nodded.

"I'll kill him . . . that bastard. I'll rip him apart." Dennis, who was all sticks and bones, and fifteen pounds lighter than I and some thirty pounds lighter than Alutto, was dead set on picking up the fight where I had left off. He headed for the door and my grandfather had to quickly grab him by the scruff of the neck to stop him from leaving the house.

"No, Dennis. There's been enough fighting for one day," said Poppy.

I pleaded with Dennis to come to his senses, but he insisted on fighting Alutto to retaliate for the beat-down I had just received. Dennis was not posturing; he had every intention of starting the battle anew. The kid was nothing but heart. No brains at the moment, but plenty of heart. Which is really all that counts.

Finally, my grandfather and I convinced Dennis to let it go . . . for now. As my grandfather patched up my face, I looked over at my brother. Despite having suffered the beating of my young life, I was grateful to have a brother so willing to put his neck on the line for my honor. I made a silent promise to myself to never let Dennis down, to be there for him like he was for me. Dennis looked at my face and saw that the bleeding had stopped.

"Good thing for Alutto you guys talked me down. I would have kicked his ass."

I smiled through my cracked lip. I was one lucky kid.

CHAPTER SIX

Tadpoles

We say that flowers return every spring but that is a lie. It is true that the world is renewed. It is also true that renewal comes at a price, for even if the flowers grow from an ancient vine, the flowers of spring are themselves new to the world, untried and untested.

—Daniel Abraham, *The Price of Spring*

Police Camp was a unique concept. Nestled in the Catskill Mountains in Tannersville, New York, Police Camp was an affordable vacation oasis with a full range of leisure activities for New York City police officers and their families. From 1972 through 1979, with perhaps but one exception, the Mulhearn clan made annual visits to Police Camp for a week-long vacation. The camp had ample outlets for all five children to amuse ourselves and provided my parents with a well-earned break from the hustle and bustle of Brooklyn. Years later I learned that my father often won a decent sum at late night poker games held long after the kids were put to bed.

One day in the Summer of 1974 stands out like no other in my childhood, for it was the day, but for the intervention of fate, my brother Dennis would have drowned.

The main building located high atop a steep hill served as a center for numerous games for kids and adults. The camp featured sports such as tennis, volleyball, and softball, as well as shuffleboard for the older folks. As much as we loved sports, however, Dennis and I were drawn mostly to the country attractions so dissimilar to the rhythm and cacophony of Flatbush Avenue. We were most fascinated by the pond located at the bottom of the hill, about half a mile from the main building and even closer to the row of bungalows which served as additional lodging for the camp's guests.

The pond was stocked with thousands of frogs and tadpoles which intrigued us to no end. We could take a fishing net, sweep it through the water and come up with a tadpole or two almost every time. The life stage of our prey was most curious and now ironic: a tadpole is the immature form of a frog or toad, after the development of its internal gills but before the appearance of its front legs and the disappearance of its tail. Like a caterpillar to a butterfly, it is caught in an odd evolutionary phase; the tadpole swims in water with its tail rather than jumps on land with the legs it will get when it morphs into a fully formed frog. More akin to a fish than an amphibian, it is very different from what it will become if allowed to grow into its final manifestation. That is a big if. Sometimes a tadpole is meant to stay a tadpole, to die as a tadpole, to never be a frog. Dennis and I, as excited nine-year-olds, gave no thought to the Darwinian consequences of our little hunt. We just wanted to catch as many frogs and tadpoles as we could.

The pond had a brick abutment at its center. About four feet high and ten feet long, the wall had a ledge no more than a foot wide which ran on its inside edge. After several hours of successful casting, our net sweeps began to come up empty. From the end of the wall, we could see that most of the tadpoles and a number of frogs had scurried away from the exposed waters and toward the safety of the brick abutment. Tired, hot, and slightly bored, I suggested to Dennis that we call it a day.

"No, Kevin, I want to catch some more frogs," he said. "Go ahead up, I'll catch up with you later."

Reluctantly, I agreed, and began the long march up the steep hill alone, without my brother. Some ten minutes later, after considerable exertion, I reached the top of the hill and saw a number of men from the bungalows start to sprint in the opposite direction, toward the lake which I had just left. "Some kid fell into the lake!" someone shouted.

Those words froze me in my tracks. I looked toward the lake but could not see anything. I could not move. I knew that Dennis had fallen into the lake and that he could not swim. My imagination started to play tricks on me. A knot formed in the pit of my stomach. Dennis had drowned. Worse still, he had drowned because I was not there to save him. I had abandoned him. My parents, who had told us to stay together, would blame me. Worse . . . far worse, I would never forgive myself. My life was ruined. My brother was gone. And it was my fault. I stayed at the top of the hill.

About half an hour later, the men who had run down the hill walked back up to their bungalows. Their shirts were stained with sweat but their faces bore no hint of what had happened or what they had just seen. They were, after all, cops. One of them locked eyes with me, though, and for just a second I saw both recognition and a hint of bewilderment stretch across his weathered face. His face spoke to me. How could this be? They just pulled you out of the lake. You must be a damned ghost.

Finally, in an act of mercy, one of the women from the bungalows screeched at her husband: "What the hell happened?"

"It's OK," the man replied. "They pulled the kid out just in time. He's gonna be OK."

I had been gifted a new lease on life. I found out later what had happened. Dennis, intent on broadening his catch, had climbed out to the ledge on the inside part of the brick wall and reached over with his net to catch some more tadpoles and frogs. He lost his balance and fell into the lake which, fortunately, was only about six feet deep. Submerged, he had the presence of mind to stick his arm up out of the water. A vacationing cop who just happened to be driving by the lake saw Dennis's arm, screeched to a halt and leapt over the brick wall. Shirtless, Dennis's rescuer—mindful that every second counted—had scraped a layer of skin off his chest when he hurdled the wall, but, bloody chest and all, this hero pulled Dennis out of the lake just seconds before my brother would have drowned. The men from the bungalows in all likelihood would not have arrived in time to save him.

That evening, when my father brought Dennis home from the hospital, he told a bunch of jokes to mask his anxiety and intense relief. He called my brother "Mark Spitz," the Olympic swimmer, and—as Dennis had chipped a front tooth in the melee—a "jack o' lantern." My mother was too shaken to even crack a grin. Her eyes were red and hollow and she was too drained to say a word. Dennis smiled shyly through his broken mouth. He was embarrassed by the attention. I don't remember what I said to him that night but I recall an overwhelming feeling of joy and gratitude engulf me. Thank you, God, for saving my brother.

Dennis was not meant to die as a tadpole.

Nor however was he destined to die an old frog.

CHAPTER SEVEN

Prince of the Sandlots

And all the winds go sighing, for sweet things dying.

—Christina Rossetti

M y father had a soft spot in his heart for a kid named Joseph Grilli, who played baseball for Kings Bay for a number of years. Joe was quick with a wisecrack or a devilish smile. He liked to razz my dad about the dominance of our Cadets teams. My father would give it right back to him, and often poked fun at the futility of Kings Bay in our head-to-head match-ups. They never could beat us, even though they featured some excellent players, like Danny Suhr, a strong-throwing and hard-hitting catcher who would star on the gridiron for Madison High School and, years later, the Fire Department of the City of New York.

The first thing a stranger noticed about Joe Grilli was that he only had one hand. Joe Grillo (no relation), my high school classmate and friend and a co-captain of Poly Prep's 1981 Varsity Football team, reminded me recently that Joe Grilli had a clean stump—probably the result of a childhood surgical procedure—just below his left wrist.

Like a mirror version of Jim Abbott, the one-armed pitcher for the Yankees, Joe Grilli was able to transfer his glove to the pocket under his left arm and, in a quick, seamless transition, pull the ball out and throw it with his one hand. He hit by resting the bat on his shoulder and flicking at the pitched baseball with his right arm. He made decent contact this way but had no power; he could barely get the ball out of the infield.

My father was not effusive in his praise for other kids, especially competitors of his teams (and sons), but his respect and admiration for Joe Grilli was transparent. This kid never complained about his physical limitations and, more importantly, always sparkled with life and a razor sharp sense of humor. Joe made sure to have fun every day he was on the planet. All of my teammates loved Joe Grilli; he was viewed not as a great kid with one hand, but simply a great kid.

Joe had a wild streak. I suppose that his parents knew that he had to be tougher than other kids to survive, so they gave him a wide berth. He had street smarts of the highest order by the time he was fourteen. He would never see fifteen. One evening, he was out late drinking and goofing around with some friends somewhere in the Sheepshead Bay area, when he decided to jump into an inground swimming pool. He dove head first into the shallow end of the pool, broke his neck, lingered in a coma for a day or so, and then died.

Had Joe survived he would have been a paraplegic. I wonder if that complete physical limitation would have broken his indomitable spirit. Knowing Joe, I doubt it.

The news of Joe Grilli's death traveled far in the sandlot circles of Brooklyn. This kid had touched and inspired many. Dennis and I asked my father to take us to Joe's wake, which was held at an Italian funeral parlor only a few miles from our home, but he refused and demanded that we complete our homework. I did not argue with him as I had no overwhelming desire to view the dead body of a fellow teenager. In hindsight, my father no doubt wanted to convey his respect and express his grief alone.

The wake of Joseph Grilli was by all accounts a remarkable event. Hundred of mourners, many of them teenagers, flocked into the Brooklyn funeral home. Scores of others spilled over into the street outside.

We found out from several teammates who had attended the wake that Joe was laid out in his Kings Bay football uniform, with his baseball uniform and cap also placed inside his coffin.

When he returned from the wake, my father came down into the basement to speak to Dennis and me. We began to pepper him with questions but he shut us down in our tracks. He then proceeded to lambaste us for about twenty minutes for our various failings. We were slobs who couldn't even pick up after ourselves. We were underachieving in school, as our grades were much lower than they should have been. We were mediocre athletes who didn't work nearly hard enough to improve our games. He left us with a sharp jab.

"That goddamn kid had more guts than the two of you put together. What do you think he could have done if he had two hands?"

When my father's tirade was over, he stormed upstairs. Dennis and I looked at each other and communicated in the silent language known only to twins who do not need words to express profound truths. Sensitive young men, we normally would have been wounded by my father's stinging criticism, but not on this night. We both understood that my father's harsh words were borne more from fear than genuine disappointment. Fear that the hand of fate could take away a child at a moment's whim. My father, a strong and tough man who had seen many a dead body on the job, looked at the effervescent Joseph Grilli lying dead in a coffin, and was forced to confront the possibility that he too could bury a child. Of course, at the time, it was only a remote possibility.

Rest in peace, Joseph Grilli, Prince of the Brooklyn sandlots.

CHAPTER EIGHT

Deck Shoes

The world is so unpredictable. Things happen suddenly, unexpectedly. We want to feel we are in control of our own existence. In some ways we are, in some ways we're not. We are ruled by the forces of chance and coincidence.

—Paul Auster

In late July 1979, our Cadets team traveled to Shore Road for the fourteen and under AABC Brooklyn championship game against a familiar foe, Gil Hodges, a team from Bay Ridge with a good mix of Italian and Hispanic ballplayers. One of its coaches was Jesse Merone Sr., and its star center fielder was Jesse Merone Jr., a teammate on several of my Poly Prep High School baseball squads.

Phil Foglietta—the iconic, larger-than-life Varsity Football Coach—was the coach of our Freshman Baseball team that year, and Jesse, John Lynch, Dennis, and I, also played for the Junior Varsity team, coached by Steve Andersen (who was Foglietta's top assistant football coach). All players on the Junior Varsity received bright, white, Poly Prep baseball jerseys, which stood out from the old, dull, gray jerseys assigned to the rest of the players on the Freshman team.

Coach Foglietta, not thrilled about having to relinquish four of his best players whenever the J.V. team played a game, branded our quartet, in a derisive growl, as the "whiteshirts."

"Hey, whiteshirts, time for you to go. Don't get those pretty goddang uniforms dirty."

Jesse Merone was a tall, strong, right-handed hitter who destroyed fastballs. His signature hit was the long, high, four hundred feet plus drive to center or left center. His problem in Brooklyn, however, was that—with no fences to keep outfielders in at a reasonable distance from home plate—many of his prodigious clouts were caught by outfielders and turned into nothing but long outs.

As our team trudged up the hill onto the Shore Road field on which our championship game would be played, some Gil Hodges players started chirping.

"Same as last year, boys, same as last year."

"Ain't nothing gonna change . . . we're still better than these guys. By a long shot."

And then, finally, the twist of the knife.

"Let's embarrass someone today, boys. Let's embarrass someone today."

The previous year, in July 1978, on this same field, we had played this same Gil Hodges team, give or take a few players, in the fourteen and under AABC Brooklyn Championship game. The game was a nightmare. We lost by a lopsided score, something like 12 to 4, and I had played atrociously. In the first inning with the game still scoreless and two runners in scoring position, a Gil Hodges batter hit an easy grounder to me at straightaway second base. The ball clanked off my glove and rolled into the outfield, which allowed two unearned runs to score. Then, after we had come back to score a few runs in our next at-bat, in the following frame I booted another grounder, which led to a big inning for Gil Hodges, after which the Cadets never seriously challenged.

On the ride back to our home, my dad lit into me. How could I have missed such easy plays? Where was my toughness, my competitiveness? What the hell had I been doing with myself every day for the last four months?

By the time we got home, my father's unrelenting verbal barrage had reduced me to a puddle of tears. Which only made things worse. Now I was a crybaby and a quitter, as well as an awful fielder and a choke-artist.

My grandfather, who—for his own self-preservation and peace of mind—had banished himself from our ballgames for at least a year, sprang to my defense.

"Jesus, Tom, why are you unloading on the poor kid?" Poppy asked.

"Because we lost, Dad, we lost bad. And this kid stank up the field," my father replied.

My grandfather told me and Dennis to go downstairs and take showers. We complied. As we trudged down the stairs to our basement bedroom, my father and grandfather started screaming at each other. My grandfather was excoriating my dad about his verbal abuse—and my father was defending himself.

A half hour or so later, after the shouting had ended and Dennis and I had both showered and dressed, Poppy limped down the stairs and entered our bedroom.

"You know, boys, you don't have to play for the Cadets," he said.

"This has to be fun for you. If it's not fun, what's the point? Winning and losing isn't everything. Playing hard, playing your best, having fun, that's what it should be about. Nothing else."

My grandfather then suggested that next year we take a break from the Cadets and play only in our local St. Thomas Aquinas Little League.

"But Dad wants to coach the Cadets; he doesn't want to coach for St. Thomas," Dennis said.

"If he doesn't want to coach you next year, I'll coach you myself," Poppy replied.

I had calmed down and regained my composure.

"No, Poppy, we want to play for the Cadets," I said. "We'll do better next year."

"OK," Poppy said, "but promise me one thing. Promise me you'll have fun and won't put too much pressure on yourselves, OK?"

Dennis and I nodded our assent and we each gave him the promise that he asked for. The crisis of the day was over.

This is the last conversation with my grandfather that I can remember. Within three months, he would be gone.

Our game in late July 1979 against Gil Hodges was a far cry from the previous year's blow-out. It was a high-scoring game where the hitters for both teams dominated the pitchers, and both teams played excellent defense.

In the bottom of the sixth inning, Gil Hodges was up a run and, with a few runners on base, was threatening to blow the game open. The Gil Hodges manager instructed his backup catcher to pinch hit, but the kid was wearing blue and white, slip-on, deck shoes, rather than baseball cleats or spikes. My father raced to the home plate umpire and argued that the kid needed to bat wearing his deck shoes; if he took the time to put on his cleats he would unduly delay the game. The umpire bought my dad's hyper-technical argument hook, line, and sneaker.

The Gil Hodges pinch-hitter, clad in deck shoes, popped up and the Gil Hodges threat had ended. But even then, the home-plate umpire did not give the kid a break and refused to let him put on his baseball cleats in between the bottom of the sixth and the top of the seventh. The back-up catcher, livid and red-faced, threw on his catcher's gear and remained in his deck shoes.

I was the third batter due up in the inning. The first two hitters made out so I was all that was standing between another crushing defeat to Gil Hodges in the Brooklyn championship game. On the first or second pitch I lined a sharp single between short and third. The Cadets were still alive.

The next batter was our first baseman, Mike Gambino, a strong, heavy kid with quick feet and hands, and a solid bat. He would eventually become the clean-up hitter for Nazareth High School. Mike was one of my best friends on the team, and I often visited him at his home near Kings Highway.

On the first pitch to Mike Gambino, the pitcher bounced a fastball and I scampered to second base. Mike then swung and missed and fouled off a pitch. It was a 1-2 count, or maybe 2-2, and my father decided to get daring. From the third base coach's box, he flashed me the steal sign.

I raced toward third on the next pitch but I didn't get a particularly good jump. The ball was high and outside, almost like a pitch out, which gave the catcher a good chance to throw me out. But, still wearing his deck shoes, the catcher's foot slipped as he threw to third and his throw sailed over the head and to the left of the third baseman and into left field. I popped up from the ground and ran home with the tying run. My Cadets teammates mobbed me at home plate.

The Gil Hodges pitcher, unnerved, walked Mike Gambino and the next batter. John Wilen, soon to be a star linebacker for Midwood High School, then crushed a three run homer to deep right-center field.

Gil Hodges still had last licks, and the Cadets—down to our third or fourth best pitcher—were trying to hang on for dear life. Gil Hodges scored a run or two and put a few runners on base with two outs. The last batter then hit a fairly long flyball to left field. Our left fielder, Kendall Mabry, slipped, staggered, and then threw his glove hand up behind his left shoulder. Just as Kendall crashed to the ground the ball settled into his glove, and he rose triumphantly with the ball in his bare hand. The Cadets were the 1979 AABC fourteen-year-old champions of Brooklyn. It was on to Ridgewood, New Jersey, for the North Atlantic regional tournament.

That evening, my entire family walked a few blocks from Kimball Street to East 36th Street for a block party. My father and mother held hands, which is one of the rare occasions I remember them engaging in a public display of affection. My father, reveling in our victory, kept paraphrasing the Gil Hodges trash talk: *"let's embarrass someone, tonight."* He must have said that line ten times, each time with an exaggerated Brooklyn paisan accent, and each time Dennis and I heard those words we cracked up. We laughed like hyenas until tears flowed freely from our eyes and our sides hurt.

Dennis and I walked ahead with an extra bounce in our steps. Sean, Deirdre, and little Thomas, just a few months shy of four, walked—with our parents—a few steps behind us.

That night, Dennis and I were so emboldened by our baseball success that we summoned the courage to ask two pretty girls to dance. And, miracle of miracles, they readily agreed. So we flashed our overbites and mechanical, rhythmless moves in the middle of the street, which had been cleared of all cars for the evening. The local band featured a lot of Bee Gees songs and other high energy disco tunes. After a few songs, we noticed that my mother had snuck down the block to observe her two oldest sons' interaction with a strange and scary breed: girls. Even this invasion of privacy did not take away from my joy that night.

Watch out, girls, I'm Kevin Thomas Mulhearn, starting, strutting, second baseman for the 1979 Brooklyn AABC Champions, the Cadets. We danced—if you could so describe our uncoordinated, semi-violent gyrations—late into the night (probably until around 9:30 p.m.).

That day, those singular twenty-four hours, was—without a doubt—the happiest day of my childhood.

I wonder what would have happened if I had struck out to end the game, or if the catcher—allowed to wear baseball spikes—had thrown me out trying to steal third.

Had I learned anything from last year's championship game debacle? Had my father, now an orphan, learned anything from Poppy? How would each of us have reacted if we had lost, if I had failed, if I had screwed up again?

Who the hell knows? But it is certainly food for thought.

I like to think, at least, that I know the answer to those questions.

CHAPTER NINE

Billy Buck

Injustice boils in men's hearts as does steel in its cauldron, ready to pour forth, white hot, in the fullness of time.

—Mother Jones

As far as accents go, Boston and Brooklyn are at the two opposite ends of the spectrum. Pak the cah in Hahvad Yahd has a regal tone; its words form a command rather than a plea; its speaker assumes an air of authority and intellectual breeding. Tro da bawl to da joik on dirty toid street, on the other hand, denotes an obvious imbecile; the listener's gut reaction is to find a wrench and a bucket of grease for his ill-bred friend to make himself at home. Of course, many a brilliant man has haled from Brooklyn and spoken with the fat oys and missing r's, and many a simpleton who sounds like a senator has called Boston his home. (Some have even served in the United States Senate). The simpleton, no doubt, is far more likely to make it big on the lecture circuit than the genius street talka from the County of Kings.

That's not why I hate Red Sox Nation.

(I want to be careful—in view of the Boston Marathon bombing in 2013—to make clear that I do not "hate" people from Boston. Many such people, no doubt, are fine, upstanding, and even exemplary individuals. When I say "I hate Red Sox Nation," therefore, I am talking merely about a prevailing mindset, a consensus point of view, rather than specific individuals. Several years ago, this caveat would not have been necessary. But, alas, as history's myriad examples of wanton death and destruction teach us, now it is).

I hate Red Sox Nation for its treatment of Bill Buckner. Yes, the man who let the slow roller trickle through his legs into short right field in the last inning of Game Six of the 1986 World Series. Ray Knight of the victorious New York Mets barreled down the third base line with the winning run, arms raised in delight like a little leaguer hitting his first home run; he was mobbed by his teammates. Buckner and the rest of his Red Sox mates slunk off the field in defeat, but only Buckner—a tough competitor, a terrific hitter for twenty-two years, a solid citizen— will carry with him the burden of that defeat, and the unfair tag of a loser, for the rest of his life.

It is not difficult to see why the City of Boston and its legion of diehard Red Sox fans turned on Buckner so viciously. The ball that Mookie Wilson hit was not struck hard, and it did not require Buckner to move much. At first glance it was the kind of routine play one expects a little league player to make, and the error was made because Buckner failed to get his glove down, which is a violation of the first principle taught to every boy who puts a mitt on his hand. The casual observer doesn't know or care that Buckner was playing despite excruciating pain in his knees and ankles, that Wilson, a speed demon, got an excellent jump out of the batter's box, and that the pitcher, Bob Stanley, got a poor start off the mound. Even if Buckner doesn't pay the toll on his play, the worst case scenario has Wilson safe at first and Ray Knight on third base with the game still tied.

So what? The fans of the Red Sox, mired in futility since 1918, had endured decades without a championship team. The Red Sox would occasionally raise the hopes of their fans but in the end they would always come up short. The Red Sox were losers, failures, but their fans had a choice to make after the 1986 collapse. They could have chalked up the loss to bad luck and misfortune, with class and dignity, or they could have taken a crasser and more venal tack. Blame it all on Buckner. If we can paint him as the symbol of failure, tag him as a loser, we will avoid having to think of ourselves as losers . . . or failures. So they took the easy route and vilified Buckner—and his family to boot—worse than any other athlete before or since. Thousands of Red Sox fans treated Buckner with the venom usually reserved for murderers and child molesters. Because he made an error and lost a ballgame. A damn ballgame.

The irrational contempt for Buckner, which many Red Sox fans prized like a battle citation, was gutless, overblown, and even misdirected. Buckner comes in a distant fifth place on my list of goats for the 1986 Red Sox. Most people overlook that the Red Sox had already blown a two run lead with two out and no runners on base by the time Buckner made his historic error. The Mets had resurrected themselves from the precipice of defeat without the slightest bit of help from Billy Buck. Calvin Schiraldi, never to be heard from again, was unable to close the door as he gave up consecutive singles to Gary Carter, born with a smile on his face, Kevin Mitchell, former gangbanger from the mean streets of Oakland, and Ray Knight, best known for being married to LPGA great, Nancy Lopez. Bob Stanley, the journeyman called on to relieve Schiraldi, was unable to finish the tenacious Mookie Wilson, who kept on fouling off tough pitches. Several times the Sox were down to their last strike. But it never came.

Stanley's penultimate pitch sailed slightly inside and handcuffed catcher Rick Gedman, a difficult pitch to catch no doubt, but one that is almost always handled by a major league catcher. Not this time. The ball clanked off Gedman's mitt and rolled to the backstop. Mitchell thundered home and stomped on home plate. Tie game. The Mets, blessed with home field advantage and incredible momentum, were not going to lose this game now. No way. Every person in Shea Stadium or watching on television, whether in Boston, New York, or elsewhere, knew in his heart that this game would eventually be won by the Mets. The only mystery left was the ending.

Then Mookie tapped his grounder to Buckner and history was made. A game which is defined by its failures more than its successes, where its all-time greats fail about seventy percent of the time, anointed its ultimate poster boy for failure. A Marlboro Man in black high-tops no less.

Buckner never even should have been on the field in that tenth inning. In prior playoff games where the Red Sox had the lead going into the last inning, Red Sox manager John McNamara had replaced Buckner at first with the more agile and able-bodied Dave Stapleton. I am convinced that he did not pull Buckner in Game Six because he wanted Billy Buck, his gamer, to be on the field for the inevitable celebration. Purely a matter of sentiment. Sentiment, unfortunately, as evidenced by the tenth inning of Game Six, has no place on the baseball field. Jonny Mac should have known better. Bill Buckner is excused if he forgets to say thank you.

When the Red Sox finally won their World Series in 2004, the Red Sox tracked down Bill Buckner at his home in Idaho, a place as far away from the mean-spirited citizens of Red Sox Nation as Buckner could get. They invited him to take part in the victory parade, to let Bostonians and the Red Sox Nation finally come to peace with Buckner and his error. To forgive if not to forget. He told them in so many words to go to hell. Bill Buckner, who asked for no one's forgiveness, was my hero.

But, no hero is perfect, and each is human. The Red Sox reached out to Bill Buckner again after they won a second World Series in 2007. This time he relented and joined Red Sox Nation in its celebration, which included a lame attempt to expiate itself from its brutal treatment of him for his historical miscue. This time Buckner ingratiated himself to the Bosox throng and accepted its embrace.

Say it ain't so, Billy Buck. Say it ain't so. Does he, or anyone else, think for one minute that Red Sox Nation would have been so forgiving, or at all forgiving, if Boston had blown both the 2004 and 2007 World Series? Buckner would still be the pariah's pariah, and he must know that deep in his soul.

So why did he accept the false, insincere, and extremely belated embrace of Red Sox Nation?

I can only guess that he got tired of being treated like a villain, and of donning goat horns in perpetuity, when all he did was make an error.

I still bristle when I hear some ignoramus pontificate that Buckner lost the 1986 Series for the Red Sox. Such confidently stated but wrong assertions always remind me that the truth, the elusive truth, often lies hidden just underneath the thin tissue of deceptions which disguise themselves as conventional wisdom.

CHAPTER TEN

Devil's Game

Throughout history, it has been the inaction of those who could have acted; the indifference of those who should have known better; the silence of the voice of justice when it mattered most; that has made it possible for evil to triumph.

— Haile Selassie

Brooklyn kids are supposed to have street smarts, if nothing else. It is the armor, unseen but omnipresent, which is expected to protect them from the harshness of the world and the cruelties of men. Practically every man I have ever met who grew up in Brooklyn recalls his place of upbringing with considerable and justifiable pride. The credo goes something like this: I was tough enough to survive the mean streets of Brooklyn, so there is now no challenge from which I will shrink, no battle I will not fight.

But not all streets in Brooklyn are mean. There is more than one oasis in the midst of the urban jungle. It is a bitter irony that one such oasis located in Dyker Heights at 92nd Street and Seventh Avenue, the venerable Poly Prep Country Day School, formed a nest from which a sexual predator preyed upon young boys for twenty-five years without penalty or sanction. As a student athlete at Poly from Autumn 1978 to Spring

61

1982, I had a front row seat, albeit with an obstructed view, to this dynamic.

The stranger to Poly Prep might ask the reasonable question: what the hell happened to those famous street smarts, not just of the kids, but of the adults charged with the education and protection of those children? To him, I would answer simply: Phil Foglietta, the revered, feared, charismatic, and highly successful football coach at Poly Prep from 1966 to 1991, could have done practically anything at Poly Prep without recrimination. For those not within the Poly family, it is impossible to understand the breadth and depth of Foglietta's power and control.

It was the gospel at Poly that Coach Foglietta used his strength and power for the most noble of purposes: to turn promising boys into successful men who would realize fully their potential. In this endeavor, there is no doubt that he often succeeded far beyond any other teacher or coach at Poly Prep. Coach, indeed, had an uncanny knack for pushing his players—with a wild yet calculated string of challenges, insults, or compliments, as the situation demanded—to achieve more, to be more, than they thought possible.

Yet even when I was a student, there was always a low but steady murmur that all was not Camelot in the world of Poly Prep. Coach Foglietta had a disturbing fondness for little boys. Especially those with blonde hair and blue eyes. One had to be blind, deaf, and dumb to not understand that, at least on some level. Many were. Many others, like me, had an inkling of Coach's Achilles' heel but would never have dreamed of acting on their suspicions for a myriad of reasons.

Still others in positions of authority knew full well of Foglietta's sexual assaults of numerous boys but were simply too afraid to make a move. Some were no doubt afraid of Foglietta himself, a menacing, powerhouse, fire hydrant of a man, quite capable of exploding into a violent rage. Many of Coach's peers or supervisors must likewise have been terrified of questioning the conduct, especially the sexual conduct, of the school's undisputed alpha male. They must have thought that if someone called out this seemingly masculine ideal as a child molester, a rapist of boys, he would flex his muscles, consolidate his power, and destroy the accuser's career as an educator.

But those who remained silent despite *knowing* that Foglietta was assaulting boys have no reasonable excuse for their inaction. This was a serial child rapist for God's sake! Someone, anyone, needed to stop him. But no one—no teacher, no coach, no administrator—ever did.

As it turns out, based on new information which was told to me by twelve survivors of Foglietta's brutality (whom I proudly represented in a notable litigation in Brooklyn federal court—*Zimmerman v. Poly Prep, CDS*),[3] the dark side of Coach's character was there all along for the powers-that-were to see. His so-called superiors were notified early in his tenure of his *illegal and immoral conduct*, not just his predilections. But this tragic situation, where boy after boy had his innocence stolen from him, was too ugly, too monstrous, for anyone to face head-on. Even now, seventeen years after Foglietta's death and after the dark and harrowing stories of my clients were published in various media outlets, in particular the *New York Daily News,* there are many who stubbornly refuse to acknowledge the reality. Phil Foglietta. Brilliant football coach. Motivator extraordinaire. Inspiration to many. Alpha male. Role model. Sexual predator. Abuser of boys. Child rapist. Destroyer of souls. I believe all of these seemingly discordant words to be true. The saga of Phil Foglietta and Poly Prep is far too complex to be confined to a single phrase.

Some of the men who engaged in willful blindness, willful deafness, or both, when it came to Phil Foglietta's conduct with children, led otherwise exemplary and laudable lives. They were educators devoted to the well-being and positive development of children. They were—often in the best sense—man makers and woman makers. Many were fundamentally decent and honest and caring and selfless. But, for some inexplicable reason, they were all paralyzed by Phil Foglietta and his power and legend into becoming de facto blockers for his too-many-to-count assaults of children.

After many years of thinking about these issues, I am *still* convinced of the core decency of many of Coach Foglietta's silent, enabling, peers, and *still* cannot make sense of how it all turned to hell. How deference to the alpha male, to Coach, trumped any sense of obligation to or responsibility for the multitude of vulnerable boys within Coach's reach.

I wish I could turn back time, transport myself back to Poly Prep circa 1978, and have a heart-to-heart talk with several of my former coaches. Two of these coaches attended my brother's wake in Manalapan, New Jersey, at the end of the Summer of 1993. The stricken, wounded look in their eyes, their visceral pain, was real. They cared about my brother. They mourned his loss. And they took the time to comfort me and my family in our darkest hour.

No one can convince me that these men did not care deeply about children. But, armed with too much knowledge, too many facts, to pretend that they remained in blissful ignorance while Phil Foglietta used Poly Prep as his personal hunting ground, I want to grab them both by their lapels and scream into their ears. You know about Coach! Do something! Stop him! Not just for the boys, but for yourselves!

But I know that it is too late for that remedy. That window has slammed shut. And that's a damn shame.

Coach Foglietta worked for a number of years as a counselor/coach at the Joe Namath Youth Football Camp in the 1970s. According to one of my former teammates, Joe Namath once heard that one of his camp members was a football player at Poly Prep. "If he plays for Phil Foglietta, he's the luckiest kid in the world," Namath reportedly said.

Maybe so, Joe . . . but only if Coach did not target him to be one of his special friends. In that case, he was left alone to battle a lifetime of guilt, shame, and distrust. These unfortunate victims, whose numbers are impossible to count, are the casualties, the detritus, of Poly Prep's football glory under Phil Foglietta—and the hefty counterweight to the hundreds of young men inspired by him to reach beyond their grasp.

The roaring crowds and multitude of backslappers and gladhanders no doubt only added to the victims' canvas of pain, especially because now they know that those who knew of the damage being inflicted and were in a position to do something about it looked away.

Go, Blue Devils! Ah, the triumph of evil does not take much. In the four years that I attended Poly, the Poly Prep Varsity Football team lost just two games and, in my senior season, defeated Lincoln High School, which was then the number one ranked team in New York City. Our football program's tremendous "success" begs the question: what price, gridiron glory?

In retrospect, every athlete who ever played for Coach Foglietta at Poly Prep should feel somewhat sullied and diminished by the revelations of Foglietta's prolonged and horrendous sexual abuse of young boys and Poly Prep's shameful cover-up. For me, the last flicker of my youthful innocence, its last ember burning, has been extinguished by my realization that at Poly Prep my perception of reality was nothing but an illusion. The glory of my youth—in which I was but a small cog for a legendary, extraordinarily successful, high school football program—was in large part a farce, a cruel joke played by a man with a multitude of talents but a fatal flaw, and enabled by his sycophants.

In the end, there is only one reasonable conclusion. Too many stepping stones. Too many casualties. Too much indifference. The sad but inescapable truth is this: Phil Foglietta, almost a great man, tragically, at his core, was also a monster. That the monster in him was allowed to run free for twenty-five years, and to pick his quarry as his appetite demanded, is a searing indictment of Poly Prep, which in the last analysis, for me, was also almost great. Emphasis, heavy emphasis, on almost.

CHAPTER ELEVEN

Crazy Legs

The dead cannot cry out for justice. It is a duty of the living to do so for them.

— Lois McMaster Bujold

On October 27, 1978, Dennis and I were about two months into our Poly Prep tenures. We were both half-backs on the Freshman Football team and vying for playing time and our own slice of gridiron glory. It was a beautiful Indian Summer day and we were playing against St. Francis Prep, my father's alma mater, resplendent in navy blue, red, and white uniforms.

Dennis and I both ran well that day. We each carried the ball about six or seven times and each had multiple runs of ten yards or more. Billy Sprance, a sophomore lineman for the Junior Varsity squad, cheered us on. After I carried the ball for a twelve yard pick-up, after a few jukes and jives, Billy yelled out, "There goes Crazy Legs Mulhearn." Our teammates laughed. Dennis and I retreated to the huddle and flashed each other a broad smile. We were beginning to make a name for ourselves at Poly and, best of all, Coach Foglietta, the school's top dog, was watching intently. Coach had been an assistant football coach at St. Francis Prep in the late 1950s (when my father had attended that school).

After the game, we showered quickly and left the locker room. As soon as we saw my father's face we knew that something was wrong. His face was ghost-white and his eyes were red and puffy.

"What's wrong, Dad?" Dennis asked.

"Get in the car, boys, I have some bad news."

As we turned to enter the back seat of my father's blue Oldsmobile, in a few seconds which seemed like an hour, I became convinced that my baby brother Thomas, who had just turned four, had died. A cloud of gloom hovered above. I was almost horrified into paralysis.

When we were settled, my father climbed into the driver's seat, twisted his body to face us, looked us in the eyes and said, "Poppy had a heart attack at the hospital early this afternoon and died."

My dad opened his mouth to say something else but no more words came out. He turned away from us and slipped the key into the ignition. For a few fleeting moments, I felt relieved that Thomas was all right. But then the enormity of Poppy's death began to sink in and my throat became constricted. My father drove away from Poly Prep. His two oldest sons sat mute in the back seat, each with a thousand yard stare, each lost in his own thoughts and deep grief.

Poppy, the man who lived for his grandchildren, the man whom we adored, the man who loved us beyond measure, was forever gone. And we didn't even get a chance to say goodbye. The unfairness of it all began growing as a pit of rancor in my belly.

Poppy was supposed to be coming home from the hospital that day. He had been in Kings Highway Hospital for about a week, diagnosed with an ulcer, treated, and scheduled to come home. My father, along with his Aunt Frances (Uncle Harry's wife), was picking Poppy up from the hospital. Poppy was about to return home to a hero's welcome as we kids had crafted several ornate "Welcome Home, Poppy" banners and hung them in our living room.

After Poppy's formal discharge, hospital rules required that he leave in a wheelchair. As my father was wheeling Poppy toward the elevator, Poppy had a massive heart attack. There was nothing the phalanx of doctors could do. My dad stood by helplessly as the life drained from his father.

My grandfather died in the early afternoon. My father returned to our Kimball Street home before heading to Poly Prep to watch Dennis and me play. According to my brother Sean, Dad's face twitched when he saw the "Welcome Home, Poppy" banners hanging in the living room. Without a word, he reached for them and crumbled them into a ball. Then he told the awful news to my mom and younger siblings and headed to the Poly football field.

Unbeknownst to me, until thirty-four years later, at the exact same time that Dennis and I were learning of my grandfather's death, the St. Francis Prep Freshman Football team was likely not having an easy time of it in the visiting team locker room.

On September 7, 2012, as I was deeply entrenched in the Poly Prep litigation, I received this anonymous email:

Mr. Mulhearn:

I recently read some articles in local publications regarding the Poly Prep scandal and your involvement as a lead attorney in the matter.

There are some avenues you should be investigating.

There is a high profile football program at St. Francis Prep in Queens. Long-time head coach Victor Davis* is well known in varsity sports. There are no allegations against him, however there was a longtime member of his staff (30 years+) who was a known pedophile. Name of Bob Stenger.

---

* This is a pseudonym.

While not as aggressive as Foglietta or a Sandusky-type, it was well known that he preyed on 14-years olds constantly. Free tickets, rides home, constant "shower monitoring."

The transition piece is this: There was a relationship between Foglietta & Stenger. It was outside the formality of the SFP program. During the late seventies/early eighties, midway through the football season, the SFP freshman football team was taken out to Poly Prep to "scrimmage" the Poly Prep team. It was done on a weekday, usually when school was off, such as a religious holiday.

But, there were no coaches involved. No administrators. No parents. Only Bob Stenger, who would use the school bus, load up the freshmen (with gear), then drive to Brooklyn. The person who greeted you at the door, was Foglietta (and then later in the showers as he and Stenger would ogle all the students).

A teenager would have never suspected what was going on. But hindsight being what it is, we now all know, there was something more latently devious.

You will have a difficult time . . . since Stenger passed away a few years back. In his last few years as a teacher, he was banished to the library and not allowed in the classroom. This was due to "suspect" behavior. There were other faculty members banished to the library (Franciscan brothers included), and some were of the same ilk.

You want to know what pisses me off the most? Why I want someone to make the connection between these two? Because the [league] had the unmitigated gall to name an award after Stenger. Could you imagine? And I know the lineage of this organization, there were many who knew what these guys were up to. So what does that tell you? They had other accomplices in the league.

The lessons of October 27, 1978, where in the County of Kings a fine man passed over into the next world and two pedophiles inflicted various indignities on a bunch of innocent adolescents: take nothing for granted, cherish every moment with your loved ones for one never knows when a beloved relative—bonded in blood—will become another ghost of October, his spectral presence remaining only in your heart and memory; the latter fading, fading over time, until nothing is left but a lingering, sometimes inexplicable or unidentifiable, feeling of love.

And the black corollary, the evil analogue, the necessary vigilance: protect your children with all your might; never assume that the authority figures in their lives are trustworthy and decent; ignore high-falutin titles and the plaudits of others; pull out all the stops to protect the tender innocence of your children.

For once it is lost, it is gone for good. That much I know.

CHAPTER TWELVE

Thumb Down

[F]or there is nothing heavier than compassion. Not even one's pain weighs so heavy as the pain one feels with someone, for someone, a pain intensified by the imagination and prolonged by a hundred echoes.

— Milan Kundera, *The Unbearable Lightness of Being*

In early December 1978, I was one of about fifteen players on Poly Prep's log-jammed Freshman Basketball team. Our "Coach" was Phil Foglietta, known throughout the metropolitan area as one of the best—if not the best—high school football coaches in Brooklyn, but not yet known to most as the serial child molester and rapist that he in fact was. Coach, deadly serious and prone to explosive fits of temper during the football season, was now a different man. Jocular, full of belly-laughs and rich, hysterical anecdotes, back-slaps, and off-key whistles, he did not remotely resemble the tyrannical control freak who prowled the football sidelines with a perpetual grimace. This season, basketball season, was rest and relaxation time for Coach. One could easily see how much he appreciated the release of pressure after a grueling gridiron season in which the Blue Devils had won every game until the finale, when—playing without its injured star quarterback, Vinny Abate—Poly suffered a heart-breaking loss to its arch-rival, St. Paul's School (from Garden City, Long Island).

But Coach did not care too much about his basketball team. Constantly kibitzing with his friends, recent alumni, or members of the football squad, it frustrated the hell out of me how little attention he paid to the daily exertions of his young team.

The games were no better, as Coach doled out playing time miserly, like a politically correct depression-era labor leader unwilling to pass anyone over for a shift. Certain that I was one of the better players on the team, it infuriated me that I usually did not play even half a game.

This December weekday, our team was scrimmaging. A player on the opposing side missed a shot and I jumped for the defensive rebound. Someone low-bridged me and I flipped backwards. Reflexively, before my head hit the hardwood, I threw out my arms to break my fall. My right hand hit the floor, thumb-first, and a moment later the rest of my body followed. The entire weight of my body, for just a split second, landed on my right thumb.

I heard the sound of a twig snapping in a forest, looked down, and saw blood spurting from my thumb, which was hanging by a thread and pointing due south instead of north.

The force of my fall had ruptured all the tendons and ligaments in the thumb on my throwing hand. My thumb had almost been severed at the knuckle. I stood there, motionless, in shock, with my thumb drooping forlornly, looking like it was about to fall off.

Coach Foglietta sprang into action. He grabbed my thumb with his meaty paw and squeezed it back into place. He instructed all the other players, including my brother Dennis, to go home. Coach marched me to his office, known as the "cage," a wire-enclosed room located in the bowels of the boys' locker room. (I learned many years later that Foglietta had sexually assaulted many Poly boys in the privacy of the "cage."). He called, in turn, a cab, my father (at his station house in the 62nd Precinct), and Dr. Soren, a top-notch orthopedic surgeon who was the father of one of my teammates. He never loosened his grip on my thumb, assured me that everything was going to be fine; he had the best surgeon in the City coming in to do my operation. I nodded blankly, mute, in severe pain, still in shock, but strangely confident that Coach would make sure that no great harm would befall me.

In a few minutes, we arrived at Victory Memorial Hospital on 92nd Street, just a few blocks north of Poly Prep. Coach again immediately took charge. He told the admitting nurse that I was to be given V.I.P. treatment as I was a promising young Poly Prep athlete, and that we were waiting for Dr. Soren to arrive to prepare for an emergency surgical procedure.

As we sat together in the waiting room, Coach continued to apply firm pressure to my thumb. A few minutes later, my dad came in wearing his NYPD uniform. Coach Foglietta, still unwilling to let go of my thumb, explained to my dad what had happened. He assured my father that Dr. Soren was the best orthopedic surgeon in the area.

"Jesus, that's his throwing hand," my father said, proving that we pretty much had the same mindset on this injury and its potential impact.

Coach nodded and began telling war stories about all the famous athletes with whom he hobnobbed. He told us that Joe Namath was his good friend, and that he worked for Namath at his youth football camp.

"I'll tell you a funny story about Joe's guarantee before the Jets won the Super Bowl.

"Ya see, that guarantee was nothing special. Joe said 'I guarantee it' all the time, it was a common figure of speech of his, a verbal tic.

"But he said, 'I guarantee it' when talking to some reporter about the game and the reporter ran with it, and Joe didn't have any chance to clarify what he meant. And the cat was out of the bag anyway. So Joe said 'what the hell' and let it go. And the rest is history."

I was mesmerized, enraptured by these stories and the colorful raconteur who told them, to the point that I didn't think too much about the excruciating pain that was emanating from my wrong-way thumb. Which was probably the point of the stories in the first place.

My father was less impressed. After Coach finally left, a good half hour after my dad arrived, my father muttered, "Damn name dropper."

But soon thereafter Dr. Soren strutted into the hospital, and—after examining my thumb—prepared me for surgery for the next day. Coach Foglietta was true to his word. Dr. Soren did an extraordinary job. The normal range of motion of a thumb for an injury like mine, post-surgery, was forty to fifty present. My thumb mobility, after I did twice the amount of the thumb-healing exercises that Dr. Soren prescribed, was close to ninety percent.

A track of tight scars line the inside of my right thumb; and now, at fifty-one, my thumb gets a bit stiff in cold weather. This scar and occasional stiffness are the only remaining manifestations of my horrific childhood injury.

Coach Foglietta took exceptionally good care of me. I was not groped or raped by this man; I was treated with considerable kindness and compassion. I cannot fathom why Coach Foglietta treated me with kid gloves, while so many of my peers, predecessors, and successors experienced the devil in this man.

Except, maybe, because my father was a cop. And, perhaps, because Coach feared the badge. And the gun.

During the Poly Prep lawsuit, I heard a third-hand anecdote that in the early 1970s a New York City police officer, whose son had told him that Foglietta was trying to get too "friendly," confronted Foglietta at Poly Prep. According to this urban legend, this police officer entered a room with Foglietta, pointed his gun at Coach's head, and advised him that if Foglietta so much as ever looked at his son funny, he would be back to blow Foglietta's brains out.

But this "fear of the gun" explanation, by itself, is too damn simple. Foglietta was a monster but he was more than *just* a monster. I'd be lying if I didn't acknowledge that there was at least a part of him that was decent and caring and genuinely concerned for the well-being of his players. I saw that side of Coach first-hand during my time at Poly Prep. And although I could be wrong, I don't think that the caring aspect of Foglietta was *entirely* a ruse and a front to enable him to continue to get away with his repugnant crimes against children.

The tragedy is that Foglietta's evil side was constantly at war with his decent side. And when the evil side prevailed, as it consistently did throughout his twenty-five year tenure at Poly Prep, it inflicted grievous, soul-shattering wounds on all who fell within its destructive path.

I don't excuse Foglietta for his reign of terror against Poly Prep students and other children. Not for a second. His conduct was as despicable as one can imagine. But I regret that his potential decency—which I personally observed in flashes—was consumed by his sick and twisted impulses. I regret that the goodness in him, the goodness which is imbued in every man and woman, was swallowed whole by his insatiable hunger to sexually assault children.

Phil Foglietta, blessed with a rare charisma and dynamic personality that made teenage boys willing to run headfirst into a wall at his command, could have been, should have been, so much more than a child rapist. And had he fulfilled his righteous destiny, had his angels beaten back his devils, the lives of the dozens (if not hundreds) of the boys he incinerated in the flame of his sick desires would have been so much happier, so much freer and unburdened, and so much more innocent.

The saga, the catastrophe, that is Phil Foglietta and Poly Prep, and the myriad survivors, and the multitude of lost boys, has far more layers than one can see with the naked eye. It cuts, in so many ways, deep into the bone.

CHAPTER THIRTEEN

Only a Junior

The crack of the bat, the sound of baseballs thumping into gloves, the in-field chatter are like birdsong to the baseball starved. [4]

— W.P. Kinsella

Toward the end of my junior year of high school, in May 1981, the Poly Prep Blue Devils Varsity Baseball team traveled to the River-dale section of the Bronx via the Brooklyn-Queens Expressway and the Major Deegan to take on the Horace Mann Lions. Unbeknownst to me until decades later, when we rolled into the Bronx, Horace Mann had an unblemished record.

Horace Mann's well-manicured baseball field was a beautiful jewel stuck, as if carved with a cookie-cutter, right in the middle of several brick school buildings which flanked the field on both the first and third base lines. A large, ornate, building, with a tall, intricately designed clock tower—I believe it was a chapel—stood just behind the high, chain-link, right field fence. In left field, some three-hundred eighty feet or so from home plate, stood an eight feet high granite wall with a gray slate top that was a few inches thick and several feet wide. When our team bus pulled into the parking lot behind the left field wall, I had no idea that I

79

was about to witness the greatest hitting performance, on any level, that I would ever see.

Although this game now exists only in the memories of those who played in or witnessed it, as there is no videotape, box score, or play-by-play description available, I remember it, give or take perhaps a few fleeting details, like it happened yesterday.

In the first inning, my brother Dennis, batting fifth or sixth, came up to the plate with two outs and runners on first and second. He crushed a fastball to right field with a smooth but violent left-handed swing. The ball continued to rise, high and far, until it disappeared over and beyond the tall clock tower behind the right field fence. This three run homer likely traveled well over four hundred feet. And Dennis was just getting started.

In his second at-bat, Dennis came up with the bases loaded and lined a sharp single up the middle, scoring two more runs. Then, several innings later, he again came up with the bases full. This time he cracked a long home run to center field, a grand slam, with the ball rolling into the small area in center where the concrete wall ended.

If you are counting, that is three at-bats, two home runs, and nine runs batted in. But the best was still to come.

In the top of the last inning, Dennis once again strode to the plate with the bases loaded. The game, as far as I can remember, was tied at twelve runs apiece. Horace Mann's pitcher, a tall, lanky right-hander with long curly hair spilling out of his cap, saw Dennis step toward the batter's box and take a nice, easy practice swing. Dennis then pointed his bat at the pitcher as was his habit.

The pitcher, an intelligent Horace Mann student, having witnessed the carnage that Dennis had wreaked the entire game, stepped off the mound and directed a pronounced shrug to his manager. *What the hell do you want me to do with this guy?*

The manager, a beefy, red-faced man, waved his arms toward his pitcher. "Get back on the mound. You'll have to pitch to him next year, too. He's only a junior."

The pitcher did as instructed, albeit with narrowed, darting eyes, and toed the rubber. His next pitch was an inside fastball. Dennis turned his hips, dropped his hands, and swung with seemingly little effort. The ball flew off the barrel of his aluminum bat like it was shot from a cannon. To this day I have never seen any high school player hit a baseball any harder. The ball, in just a few seconds, caromed off the metal right field fence with a loud clank. This line drive, this missile, never had a chance to descend and still hit about twelve feet high up the chain-link fence. Dennis hustled into second base with a thunderous double and two more RBIs, for a grand total of eleven for the game.

Horace Mann, desperate to finish a perfect season, did not die quietly. In their last at-bat, one of their players smoked a long home run to left field, a prodigious shot, over the concrete wall. The Lions then put runners on first and second. With two outs, Horace Mann's final batter hit a line drive to center field which, if it dropped in for a hit, would have tied the game. But it was not to be. This was Dennis's game. Our speedy center fielder, Vinny Sangiovanni, raced in and made a difficult shoe-top catch to end the game.

When the ballgame was over, Dennis sat in the back of our bus, which we shared with the girls' softball team, like a conquering hero. Even the star seniors, Peter D'Agostino, Vinny Sangiovanni, and Mike D'Ambrosia, treated him with deference. Four hits in four at-bats, two home runs, and eleven RBIs in one game! Jesus Christ, Mulhearn, what the hell got into you today?

I sat down next to my brother and he flashed me a huge smile. "I just knew I was going to crush that ball the last time up," Dennis said. "I didn't think it. I knew it."

I smiled back at him. I now knew that I could not match my brother. This game clinched our long-running debate and intra-twin competition: Dennis was indisputably the best baseball player in our family. But I could live with that. On the bus, Dennis glowed with pride and was unable to suppress his broad, toothy smile. I had never seen my brother so content.

Horace Mann finished the 1981 season with a record of twenty-two wins and one loss. If not for Dennis's remarkable slugging performance, Horace Mann would have completed a perfect season. Decades later, though, I discovered that there was more, much more, to the story. The world of Horace Mann was far from perfect.

Horace Mann's manager was a man named R. Inslee Clark Jr., known to friends as "Inky." He was Horace Mann's headmaster and a highly regarded educator, renowned for fostering racial and gender equity and diversity. But, it seems, he was also both a pedophile and a pedophile enabler.

I first heard about Inky Clark when reading Amos Kamil's groundbreaking article in the *New York Times Magazine,* "Prep School Predators" (June 6, 2012), which exposed the underbelly of widespread sexual abuse at Horace Mann from the 1960s through the 1980s. Amos graduated from Horace Mann in 1982 (the same year Dennis and I graduated from Poly Prep) and had starred at second base for the Lions in 1981 and 1982. Like my brothers and me, Amos's ticket to an elite prep school education was his baseball prowess.

Amos Kamil's 2012 article sent shock waves through the Horace Mann community because it pinpointed both the incredible prevalence of the sexual abuse of Horace Mann students by faculty members, and, just as troubling, if not more troubling, many school administrators' shocking indifference to multiple reports of sexual assaults against children by various Horace Mann teachers and coaches.

After specific complaints of sexual abuse had been made to several Horace Mann officials about several prominent teachers, Horace Mann took no action, and thus permitted several known sexual predator faculty members to remain on staff at Horace Mann for years, free to continue to abuse more unsuspecting children.

In his *New York Times Magazine* article Amos Kamil did not directly accuse Inky Clark of sexual abuse but recounted in vivid detail an evening where Clark and a Horace Mann history teacher, Stanley Kops, who was eventually fired from Horace Mann for sexual misconduct, took him, his younger brother, and a friend, to dinner in New York City. Implicit in this story was Amos's speculation that maybe, on that night, in which alcohol poured freely and various teacher-student boundaries were crossed, Amos, his brother, and his friend, had all dodged a bullet.

Amos Kamil's article spurred a group of concerned Horace Mann alumni intent on obtaining full disclosure of the facts and a measure of justice for the Horace Mann survivors—The Horace Mann Action Coalition—to hire the Honorable Leslie Crocker Snyder, an esteemed former New York City prosecutor and judge, to conduct an investigation into sexual abuse at Horace Mann. The Horace Mann School itself refused to cooperate with her probe.

After months of inquiries and interviews with former students and faculty members, in the last week of May 2015, Judge Snyder released her report: *"Making Schools Safe: An Investigation into sexual abuse at the Horace Mann School, with recommendations for how independent schools can protect our children."*

A transcript of statements of several Horace Mann survivors at an April 22, 2013 press conference is annexed to the back of the report (as Appendix 9). One of the speakers at that press conference, John Snyder[†], who graduated from Horace Mann in 1979, claimed that when he was fourteen, Inky Clark and Stanley Kops (the same teacher who joined Amos Kamil, *et al.* for a night on the town more than five years later),

---

[†] This is a pseudonym.

after plying Snyder with alcohol, picked up two young male prostitutes in New York City and forced Snyder to engage in sexual acts with them. Then, when the male prostitutes left, Clark and Kops continued to sexually abuse Snyder.

According to John Snyder, over the next several years, on about five occasions, Inky Clark directed Snyder to his house and then sodomized him. Snyder also stated that he was sexually abused by eight different Horace Mann faculty members.

I'm quite certain that Amos Kamil, a spirited defender and advocate for his victimized classmates and fellow alumni and a man who puts children first, realizes full well how lucky he was to escape a school led by Inky Clark with his body and spirit still inviolable. [5]

One more side note: Poly Prep's third base coach in Dennis's epic game against Horace Mann was none other than Phil Foglietta. I wonder what Clark and Foglietta talked about after the game.

Part Two:

Sunset

It's so much darker when a light goes out than it would have been if it had never shone.

— John Steinbeck, *The Winter of Our Discontent*

CHAPTER FOURTEEN

A Player, Not A Coach

In order to disobey, one must have the courage to be alone, to err and to sin. But courage is not enough. The capacity for courage depends on a person's state of development. Only if a person has emerged from mother's lap and father's commands, only if he has emerged as a fully developed individual and thus acquired the capacity to think and feel for himself, only then can he have the courage to say "no" to power, to disobey.

— Erich Fromm, *On Disobedience*

On a bitterly cold afternoon in late April 1983, the Muhlenberg College Mules Baseball team played a home game, in Allentown, Pennsylvania, toward the end of our mediocre season. I don't remember the team we played or the outcome of the game. I remember that during this game I challenged the will of an authority figure. As the oldest child of a strong-willed, dominating, New York City police officer father, I had been taught to respect my elders and do whatever was asked of me.

But on this day, for some reason, I decided to assert my own will. It was an early inning, maybe the bottom of the first, and I was sitting on my usual spot on the bench, shivering beneath my too light windbreaker, and focused not on the game but on staying warm. Coach Sam Beidleman, a gruff, stocky man with a football background and mentality, headed for the third base coaching line, his normal location, and noticed that none of his bench players had headed to the first base coaching line.

Throughout my freshman season, as I sat behind the senior first baseman, Gary Greb, and struggled for some way to make a contribution, I had often volunteered to be the first base coach.

Coach Sam, seeing the vacancy at first base, bellowed, "Bucko, we need you at first. C'mon let's go."

I hesitated for a split second, then stood up, and yelled back, "Coach, I'm a player, not a coach!" I then sat back down on the bench.

Jesse Merone, my teammate at Poly Prep, who unlike me had an auspicious start to his Muhlenberg baseball career, looked at me and turned his palms to the sky. What the hell are you doing?

Coach Sam, not used to being defied, became irate. One could almost see the steam coming out of his mouth and nose. He directed another player to man the first base coaching line. After the inning, he approached the bench, still irate, and berated me in front of the entire squad for my defiance, only now I was called "Mulhearn," not "Bucko." I don't think Coach Sam called me "Kevin" or "Bucko" for the rest of the year. I was now "Mulhearn" and "Mulhearn" with disdain.

Just a few days later, on a much warmer afternoon, the Albright Lions (from Reading, Pennsylvania) rolled into Muhlenberg. When the Lions' bus stopped in front of the field, my brother Dennis was one of the first players to depart. He was Albright's starting right fielder. Soon thereafter, I saw my dad, mom, sister Deirdre, and brother Thomas, walk behind the field and set up folding chairs. I felt slightly humiliated knowing that my family had traveled from Brooklyn to see this game, to see Dennis and me play against each other, when, especially in view of my recent "I'm a player not a coach" declaration, it was extremely unlikely that I would ever get off the bench (except, perhaps, to be first base coach).

But Coach Sam surprised me. "Mulhearn, come here," he said, minutes before first pitch. "You're playing first and batting seventh," he snarled.

I had a good game. I went two for four, with a line drive up the middle and a well-placed grounder between short and third, but what stands out for me about this game was my reaction to seeing my brother at the plate and on base.

In his first at-bat, Dennis walked. When he touched first base his game face was on. Scott Garfield, our pitcher, appreciating the rarity of the situation, made several half-hearted pick-off attempts to me at first base. When I applied a belated tag on Dennis's hip, I whispered, "You're out." Dennis's veneer cracked for a second and he smiled broadly. Then his game face went back on.

Our fun and games ended when the next batter hit a slow ground ball to our shortstop, Dale Weiss. Dennis ran as fast as he could to second base and arrived just a second after the throw. He barreled into our second baseman, Tim Hall (from Ramsey, New Jersey), with an aggressive football rolling block, shoulder connecting squarely to hip, which knocked Tim to the ground. When Tim picked himself up, gingerly, ball still in glove, he shot Dennis an angry glare. Dennis tipped his hat. I did not think Tim would be fool enough to escalate the encounter. Tim turned away and dusted off his pants.

I looked over behind home plate and saw my father beaming with pride. There is a right way and wrong way to play baseball. The right way requires both hustle and toughness. Dennis had been taught the right way to play baseball. That was no longer in doubt.

In a late inning, with the Mules nursing a slim lead, Dennis came up with two outs and a few men on base. For the first and only time in my life, I was rooting for my opponent to get a hit. Dennis crushed a fastball on the outside edge of the plate and rocketed a hard line drive to deep left field. Scott Cooperman, an infielder playing out of position in left, took off in wild pursuit of the ball. Scott was not a natural ballhawk or a particularly good outfielder, but on this play he resembled Willie Mays. Running in a sprint for some seventy or so feet, Scott leaped at the last second and caught the ball in the webbing of his outstretched glove.

It was an incredible game-saving catch. And I was crushed with disappointment for my brother. When Scott held up his glove in triumph, Dennis kicked the dirt between first and second, ala Joe DiMaggio.

The Muhlenberg Mules hung on to win this game, 10 to 7. I realized on that day that the bond between my brother and me was far stronger than any bond between me and my teammates, or me and any other person or group. I was a twin first, a Mulhearn second, and a Mule third. Nothing would ever change that pecking order.

CHAPTER FIFTEEN

Southern Comfort

Ah, it's my longing for whom I might have been that distracts and tor-ments me!

— Fernando Pessoa, *The Book of Disquiet*

In the Summer of 1983, after our freshman year of college, Dennis and I worked as waiters in a Virginia Beach Howard Johnson's hotel that boasted a beautiful ocean view. I had secured these jobs for us during my spring trip as a member of the Muhlenberg College Varsity Baseball team. On the night before a scheduled day game in Virginia Beach, the team pulled into our hotel's parking lot. Later, as we explored Virginia Beach in the middle of March, it was a virtual ghost town. Despite the near solitude, I was able to envision a summer scene right out of a Hollywood movie studio. Here was the place I would meet the girl of my dreams and fall in love, all the while stuffing the freely parted money of scores of tourists into my pockets. Impulsively, I cornered the manager and pitched him about the two experienced waiters from Brooklyn who were eager to start work once the school term ended. I didn't mention that Dennis and I had been banquet waiters only and had never worked a table service job. No matter, the manager liked my Brooklyn moxie and hired us on the spot. My teammates laughed at me. They thought I was crazy. They had no concept that to me—a kid from

Flatbush Avenue in Brooklyn—Virginia Beach was as alluring as a Caribbean paradise.

While Dennis and I were enthusiastic about the job, we were not exactly poster boys for preparation and organization. We showed up in Virginia Beach right after the big Memorial Day weekend with about a hundred bucks between us and no place to live. Some kind soul directed us to Angie's Hostel, a friendly place run by a sweet lady who catered to itinerant travelers like ourselves. The hostel advertised to foreign visitors and had guests from Sweden, Germany, and England, to name but a few ports of origin.

On the first night in Virginia Beach, Dennis and I stayed up until the wee hours talking about a range of topics: school, baseball, our family, and, last but not least, girls. Soon we were joined by a German by the name of Frank Schmidt; he was cocky bordering on arrogant, and, despite that he was about thirty-five years old and missing three fingers on his right hand, it became apparent that he had just had sex with an eighteen-year-old girl named Theresa, who was endowed with a pretty smile and enormous breasts. Frank and Theresa were giddy in a post-coital kind of way and took a liking to the two twins from Brooklyn.

Soon we had made arrangements to room for the summer with Frank Schmidt in a small apartment about five blocks from the beach and about half a mile from the Howard Johnson's in which we would be working. After about three days, Frank tired of Theresa but she refused to take no for an answer. Eventually, after Frank persuaded Theresa that their relationship was a figment of her imagination, she turned her attention to me. One night she and I groped each other in the living room after we wrongly presumed that Dennis and Frank had fallen asleep. Frank moved past the living room to go to the bathroom. He surveyed the scene of two near naked teenagers fumbling and thrashing about and chortled, "so much for true love."

At least he was off the hook. Theresa soon moved on to another guy with much more carnal experience than I. And, for about six weeks, that was the end of the beach romances for the Mulhearn brothers. Too much work. Too much sleep. Not enough stones. We talked openly about our futility.

"We have to go for it more, Kev, just make it happen," lamented Dennis.

"I know . . . I know . . . we need to be more aggressive," I replied.

"Look around, Kev, all these other guys are scoring left and right and they don't have half of what we have."

We vowed, from that day forward, to pursue the attractive girls with vigor and confidence. Within the next few nights we were put to the test. Howard Johnson's had the good sense to hire a new ice cream girl, Julia,[‡] a pretty blonde with a cute, curvy body. Upon the introductions, she smiled at us and lit up the room.

"You guys must be from Noo Yawk," she mocked us in a good-natured way. "I just love the way you'all talk." Dennis and I looked at each other. This was the opening we had been looking for all summer. The only problem was that there were two of us and just one of her. The rest of the evening turned into a scene from a bad Charlie Chaplin movie. Dennis and I would each serve our tables and then rush back to Julia for a little flirtatious banter. A smile here . . . a laugh at one of our bad jokes there. She was definitely digging us but we were like two horses racing for the wire, each taking turns at poking our necks in front. Finally, as the closing hour approached, I made my final push for the lead.

"What do you say we take a walk on the beach after we get outta here?" I asked. I knew her answer before she said anything; her smile quickened my pulse.

That night I learned how to connect to a woman in a meaningful way. Under the black sky and bright stars, amidst the roar of the ocean,

---

[‡] This is a pseudonym.

Julia and I looked deeply into each other's eyes, kissed with passionate intensity, hugged and groped each other with enough fervor to make it clear that our bodies belonged together, and talked about seemingly every important topic imaginable. When we finally pried ourselves apart at about five in the morning, I practically skipped home. I had found a girlfriend and maybe a woman to love. I could close my eyes and taste her, smell her, feel her.

I thought at that precise moment that I knew everything I needed to know about Julia. In reality, I knew nothing. Nothing.

I was shocked to see that Dennis had waited up for me. It was obvious that he was smashed. Normally not a heavy drinker, he had polished off almost an entire bottle of Southern Comfort. He stared at me with his bloodshot eyes with a look that is seared into my memory. Not angry, really, but devastated, disappointed. His eyes said, how could you do this to me, Kevin? He shook his head in disgust, tossed the empty bottle of booze on the couch, and stumbled into the bedroom.

I didn't give this a whole lot of thought at the time . . . all's fair in love and war and all that, but thirty-two years later the question haunts me. Especially because only recently I have received some new, disturbing, and profound revelations about Julia.

The thing I disliked most about Julia was her hair. It was a pleasant shade of dirty blonde, but cut short, pixie-style, it never even covered her ears. When I looked at Julia from the back, I didn't see a glamorous woman with flowing, sensuous locks that invited me to ravage her. I saw a girl who looked like a boy. For Julia, though, her shorn hair was emblematic not of a poor style choice but of an ongoing tragedy. I suggested several times that she let her hair grow long and her response was always the same: a withering stare that made me want to quickly change the topic.

Unbeknownst to me, Julia had worn her hair long as a child. The adopted daughter of a Navy officer and his wife, who resided in Virginia

Beach when he was not out to sea, Julia's daddy loved her long hair. Loved to stroke his fingers through her tresses . . . until one day the Navy officer decided to caress not just Julia's hair, but the special parts beneath her hair, the parts reserved for someone she was supposed to love, someone who was supposed to take care of her.

But the Navy officer didn't care about all that. He made her do things to him that are unimaginable and unspeakable. His sexual abuse of Julia went on throughout her childhood. The Navy officer did not discriminate; he likewise abused his adopted son (who was a few years younger than Julia).

The nadir of Julia's nightmare occurred when her mother walked into a bedroom while the Navy officer was abusing her. Julia's mother became enraged but, perversely, the target of her wrath was not her pedophile husband, but the young girl who induced his sin.

A day or two after her revolting discovery, during a pool party with neighbors and their children, Julia's mother waded into the pool where the children were swimming, grabbed Julia by her long, flowing hair, called her a slut and a whore, and pushed Julia's head under water until she was gasping for breath. The adult neighbors interceded and pulled Julia's mother off of her daughter and dragged Julia out of the pool. Her mother then grabbed Julia by the arm, screamed at her neighbors to mind their own fucking business, and dragged Julia into the house. Once safely inside, she reached for the scissors, yanked Julia's hair one last time, and then chopped it—like a deranged Sweeney Todd—close to the scalp.

In the Spring of 1987, I visited the sprawling campus of Virginia Tech (in Blacksburg, Virginia), Julia's college, to try to rekindle our romance. She told me that her brother had recently punched her father in the face and broken his jaw. I thought her brother an ingrate and never fathomed that he was more than justified in his assault on the abuser who claimed to be their father.

That first night, as we were lying in bed, but before we had removed any clothes, Julia told me that she had been dating a guy named Dennis and that she and I were better off as friends. The kiss of death. She unceremoniously kicked me out of her bedroom. I was so shallow at the time that I tried to hit on Julia's suite mate, a gorgeous blonde. Fortunately for all involved, my clumsy pass was not reciprocated.

Julia eventually married this Dennis. They have two sons, one of whom battles a mild form of autism, and Julia has struggled for years with manic depression. The last time I talked to her, more than five years ago, she revealed to me the dark secrets of her adolescence. I sensed how much the ongoing fight to maintain mental and emotional stability had taken out of her. Her father has long been gone and her mother has recently joined him in death, but the ghosts of her childhood still torment her. I was so poorly equipped to deal with any issues of emotional depth when we were dating. I always saw the highs but never looked hard enough to see the lows.

My brother Dennis would have been able to see these lows. He may have actually been the Dennis she was supposed to marry. Julia was a survivor forced to confront a deep, dark place in her own subconscious, her own soul. She may have been my brother's bedrock, his salvation, and, in turn, he may have been her stepping stone to peace.

After Julia told me her horrific story, I was left with unanswerable but nagging questions: Did I steal the woman who should have been the love of Dennis's life? Would she have been able to save him? Would he have been able to make her happy and help overcome the pathos that was her childhood? Why did I elbow Dennis to the side when a bona fide opportunity for romance presented itself?

When I think about it long enough, I wonder if perhaps I was like a stick stuck between the spokes of two beautiful and shiny bicycles, an unwitting catalyst for sending both of them to the ground.

CHAPTER SIXTEEN

The Sweet Spot

Baseball is continuous, like nothing else among American things, an endless game of repeated summers, joining the long generation of all the fathers and all the sons.

— Donald Hall, *Fathers Playing Catch With Sons*

In my sophomore year at Muhlenberg College, Gary Greb had graduated, so the first base job was wide open. That winter I had embarked on an intense weight-lifting regimen. I pounded the weights almost every day and then played full court pick-up basketball games at the gym. I reported to the Mules' Baseball team in the best shape of my life. Once we began to take batting practice the results of my new twenty pounds of muscle were apparent. The ball was jumping off my bat and I was driving the ball from foul line to foul line.

When our season began in Virginia and North Carolina, during spring break, I had managed to fend off Rob Endres, a sophomore from a nearby Pennsylvania town, and Tom Moyer, a tight end on the football team who became one of Coach Sam's favorites, to claim the job as starting first baseman. But the spring trip quickly became a disaster for me. Facing pitching that was no better than the kind I clobbered in high school, my swing fell apart and I could not get the ball out of the infield. My outs were weak: mostly tepid pop-ups and the occasional dribbler to the pitcher. By the end of the trip, my classmate Rob Endres had claimed the first base position (and he held that position until we graduated in 1986). I returned to Muhlenberg—after warming the bench for the last three games we played down south—both crestfallen and irate at myself for not making a better showing. I was better than that ... I knew it, but thought I might never get another chance to prove myself to Coach Sam and my teammates.

After we returned north, one of our first games was against a New Jersey college in Elizabethtown. Before batting practice, I grabbed a bat and took a few practice swings. My teammate, Steve Flatko, the only commuter on our team—and thus very much an outsider—approached me.

"Why are you holding your bat so damn high?"

"What the hell are you talking about?" I replied.

He then showed me that I was holding the bat parallel with my ears, about six inches higher than optimal (just below the shoulders). This was causing me to hitch when I swung, which deprived me of all bat speed and power.

I knew immediately that Steve had figured out my hitting problems. I also recognized an easy truth. None of the Muhlenberg coaches had said a word about the position of my hands or bat. My father, a master hitting technician, would have corrected this obvious and serious hitting flaw in about five seconds. But Dad was in Manalapan, New Jersey (where my family had moved that past summer), not Allentown, so I was on my own.

During batting practice before the game in Elizabethtown, I made the swing correction and dropped my bat into proper hitting position. The results were immediate. I sprayed line drives all over the field (including a few over the fence) and, when done, looked over to see if Coach Sam had noticed. I couldn't tell.

In the last inning we were down about six runs. With one out and no one on, Coach Sam told me to grab a bat and hit for Akhy. As I walked to home plate, I crossed paths with Akhy Khan, my classmate and our star shortstop (he had hit two home runs in our last game the previous year). Akhy, ticked at losing an at-bat, slammed down his bat and flipped his helmet off in disgust.

When I approached home plate I kicked up some dirt and rubbed it on my hands. Then I stepped into the batter's box and dug in my back heel. I held my bat away from my body, just below the shoulders, and waited to attack the first good pitch. I swung at a fastball just a bit toward the inside corner and made solid contact. For a few seconds, as I watched the ball soar toward left center field, I thought I may have gotten enough of it for a home run. But I had just missed it; missed the sweet spot by about a quarter of an inch. The center fielder drifted back about ten steps and caught my flyball a few steps in front of the warning track. A few minutes later, when the last out was made, my teammates and I marched into the visiting team's locker room.

I took my time getting into the showers and lingered in the warm water for as long as I could. As I was still getting dressed, Coach Sam yelled for us to head for the bus. I scrambled to catch up with my teammates and trudged behind with my hair still wet.

After the sun went down, the cold air of New Jersey in early spring crept in and the late March wind blew hard into our faces. The parking lot was almost a mile away from the locker room so we walked outside for at least fifteen minutes. By the time I entered the bus—the last man in—I was shivering. Even though the bus was heated, I could not shake the chills. By the time we returned to Muhlenberg, I had a fever.

The next morning, still feverish, I stayed in bed and pulled the blanket over my head. At noon or so, my roommate, Ernie Deeb, a nursing student at Cedar Crest College, put his hand on my forehead.

"Jesus, you're burning up," he said.

By this time, in addition to the high fever, I had a persistent, rattling cough. Ernie made me get up and get dressed. He wrapped a blanket around me, escorted me to his truck, and drove me to the school infirmary.

The infirmary, an isolated medical facility for Muhlenberg students, was not much of an improvement from my fraternity bunk. A few hours later, though, in the late afternoon, a doctor came by, examined me, and took some X-rays. After he reviewed the X-rays, he came back and told me that I had a bad case of pneumonia.

"When can I play ball again, doctor?" was the first thing I asked.

He looked at me and smiled.

"You don't understand what I just told you. You have a serious illness. You'll be out of school for at least three weeks and when you return to classes you'll have to be extra careful for at least another month. No heavy exertions. No outside running. Otherwise, you could easily relapse. And trust me, you don't want that to happen."

"So, what you're telling me is that my season is over?"

"Yes. That's what I'm telling you. I'm sorry. Just concentrate on getting better."

The doctor's words caused me to drift into a deep depression. For the next few days, my fever kept spiking to above 104 degrees. The doctor called my parents, updated them on my condition, and implored them to pick me up and take me home. My father picked me up that evening, armed with three heavy blankets for the two hour trip back to Manalapan.

On the ride back my father frequently checked the rear view mirror to make sure that I was still breathing. My chronic hack of a cough provided some evidence that I was down but not out. When I saw his darting eyes, reflected from the rear view mirror, I saw the eyes of a man who was extremely concerned about his son's health. I saw in his steel blue eyes the deep love of a father for his son. He did not need to mouth the words. His eyes, slightly glassy and narrowed into a squint, did all the talking for him.

Toward the end of the trip, as we neared our house, I sat up and talked to my father.

"My season's done, Dad. I think I'm finished."

My father, who dreamed that one of his sons would make it to the Major Leagues, who talked in a unique language of baseball metaphors, who was consumed by all things baseball until the day he died, turned his head around to face me.

"That doesn't matter, Kevin. That's not important now. What's important is that you rest up and get better."

Slowly but surely, after I returned to the loving, tender care of my mother—armed with a dozen different ways to make chicken soup—I began to heal. I stayed home and convalesced in Manalapan for about a month.

When I returned to Muhlenberg in April, I was still quite weak. I had lost the twenty pounds of muscle that I had gained in the winter and my atrophied legs made it difficult for me to do even simple things like climbing stairs. I returned to classes but avoided the baseball field. Not once for the remainder of the season did I visit my teammates or coaches. I had decided that—even after I fully recovered—my baseball playing days were over.

My statistics for the 1984 baseball season were downright ugly. Twelve at bats. Zero hits. One last long flyball to center field. One crippling case of pneumonia.

But my take-away from that year was nevertheless positive. I was surrounded by people, my family, who loved me dearly. And my father, my old-school, tough old man of a father, loved me even though he knew—for sure now—that I was not going to be the next Mickey Mantle, or even the next Fred Stanley. I did not have to star on the baseball diamond to win my father's love. It was unconditional. I could see it in his eyes when he had repeatedly peered into the rearview mirror to make sure that I was still breathing.

Despite his deeply ingrained Irish stoicism and his inability to verbalize his feelings and emotions, I was now absolutely certain that my dad loved me and would always love me, no matter what I did or did not do with my life. No matter whether I failed or succeeded in my goals. That knowledge, that certainty, born at the time my baseball career died, was, and remains, a precious gift.

CHAPTER SEVENTEEN

Sun Delay

Some painters transform the sun into a yellow spot, others transform a yellow spot into the sun.

— Pablo Picasso

In the late Spring of 1987, a few months before I started law school, I watched a bunch of my kid brother Thomas's baseball games in the Manalapan, New Jersey Little League. Thomas played for the Giants, which had sharp green and yellow uniforms, for a coach named Herb, a super nice guy who, to be kind, lacked my father's baseball acumen. But Herb had a positive attitude and cared a great deal about his kids. Thomas played quite well that season. He was his team's number two pitcher and, with a smooth left-handed swing, had a hot streak toward the end of the season where he hit nothing but line drive after line drive.

But these games were an ordeal, pure torture really, for my father, who managed his last sandlot game in which Dennis and I played in 1982. My father had left the Cadets that year because of a silly dispute with a Cadets administrator over some perceived slight, so in our last year playing on the sandlot fields of Brooklyn we were forced to wear the hideous yellow and black colors of the Gravesend baseball organization. That year, most of the Cadets players from the prior season stayed loyal to my dad and made the switch with us from the Cadets to Gravesend, but their loyalty didn't last too long. By mid-season the name of our team became a self-fulfilling prophesy and we began to regularly forfeit games because most of the players on our team of seventeen-year-olds had better things to do than play baseball all day every weekend. Some of our opponents and even a few umpires lamented the ignominious end of the champion Cadets, now disguised as bumble, or bumbling, bees. After dominating the Marine Park League and the rest of the Brooklyn sandlot leagues for eight seasons, in 1982 we went out with a distinctive whimper, not a bang.

But our Cadets teams had nevertheless set a high standard that Thomas's Giants team, and the Manalapan Little League itself, could never live up to in my father's eyes. And he let everyone in earshot know about it. The Manalapan Little League was pathetic. The players were soft and lazy. The play was grossly inferior. The umpiring was atrocious. All things baseball in Manalapan were second-rate compared to our stalwart Cadets teams, for which the legend had already begun to swallow the facts.

During one game in which Thomas was pitching for the Giants, my dad believed that the home plate umpire was squeezing the strike zone, so my father began, in his inimitable style, to sharply criticize his calls on balls and strikes. The young umpire, just a teenager, soon had enough of my father's scathing verbal abuse, walked toward my dad, and said, "Mister, if you think this is so easy, why don't you take my equipment and umpire the game yourself." But he had challenged the wrong man. My father immediately marched onto the field, grabbed the mask from the kid umpire and said, "let me show you how it's done, kid," and proceeded to umpire the rest of the game. As my father believed that the strike zone for youth baseball should be pretty big, I'm sure that Thomas, as well as the pitcher on the opposing team, got the calls on more than a few borderline pitches.

The low point of that Little League season occurred, I think, in late May or early June. The game was moving along smoothly until the manager of the team in the field waved his players into their dugout. Both teams then sat impassively in their dugouts for about ten or fifteen minutes. My father, who was watching the game from a good location in the outfield, couldn't control himself. He walked toward the Giants' dugout and asked Herb why the game had been delayed. My dad did not like Herb's answer.

"A sun delay! A goddamned sun delay!" my father bellowed. "You've got to be kidding me! What are you doing to these kids? What are you turning them into?"

Herb told my dad that it was a safety issue. The bright sun was setting directly behind the pitcher's mound and the batters were blinded by the sun and could not see the baseball as it approached home plate.

My father was still not satisfied with the explanation and continued to rant and rave about how the Manalapan Little League coaches were turning these kids into a bunch of marshmallows.

"If I tried to pull this stunt in Brooklyn, they would have thrown me out of the league," he shouted. "And they would have been within their rights."

As I sat in the stands watching this high comedy unfold, I was struck by how closely my father resembled his own father when Poppy had watched us play in Marine Park but could never manage to keep quiet and refrain from railing against the various injustices inflicted against us.

I could understand my father's aggravation over the sun delay, as I agreed that it was ridiculous, but I didn't understand why my father would get so worked up about it. There was no good reason for my father to become so enraged over such a small and inconsequential incident.

But then it hit me like a brick to the skull. My father was at that time a most unhappy man. He was miserable in his own skin.

I was not wrong about this. A few months later, in September 1987, during my first few weeks as a student at the Villanova University School of Law, my father left our house, separated from my mother, and moved in with the woman who would eventually become his second wife: "Willie," short for "Awilda."

Thomas did not respond well to my parents' separation, which occurred in fits and starts, with my father leaving, coming home, leaving, coming home again, and then leaving for good. That year, extremely depressed over the domestic turmoil in our home, Thomas put on about forty pounds. This weight gain severely damaged Thomas's baseball future, especially because his high school's Freshman Baseball coach was a running fanatic who ran his players until they dropped. Thomas struggled with all the running and was cut from the Freshman team.

Over the next few years, Dennis, Sean, and I tried to teach Thomas the finer points of baseball and resurrect his once promising career, but it was just never the same for my kid brother when our father exited the picture. Gone with my father was Thomas's enthusiasm for playing ball.

Both Thomas and my sister, Deirdre, who as a girl could not play baseball, drew the short straws when it came to their relationships with my father. Without baseball as an ever-present bridge, it was exponentially more difficult for my father to communicate his thoughts and feelings to my youngest brother and sister. Dad spoke primarily in the language of baseball. Dennis, Sean, and I, immersed in the game and first-hand witnesses to my dad's baseball passion, understood that language well. Thomas and especially Deirdre, however, both occasionally needed a translator. My father did not realize, until just before the end of his life, that maybe, just maybe, it would have been a good idea for him to try and learn a second language.

CHAPTER EIGHTEEN

Nasty Boys

Wherever you go in the next catastrophé
Be it sickroom, or prison, or cemet'ry
Do not fear that your stay will be solit'ry
Countless souls share your fate, you'll have company!

— Roman Payne, "The Basement Trains"

October 20, 1990

It was our twenty-sixth birthday. I was living in a swanky one bed-room apartment on the Upper East Side of Manhattan, a perk of my new job as an associate at a top-tier Park Avenue corporate law firm. In the span of sixty days I had morphed from a flat broke palooka into a hot shot novice lawyer with a starting salary close to six figures. I had not yet begun to resent the tediousness and pointlessness of many of my assign-ments, that I was usually representing the guy—or more often the corpo-ration—in the black hat, or the mind-blowing snobbery and sense of entitlement of many of my peers. No, I was too blind, too dazzled, to rec-ognize that I was a bridge and tunnel guy wading through an environ-ment that would prove to be most hostile and cause much damage. For now, I was enjoying the good life, eating out every evening, always tak-ing a taxi rather than public transportation, and dreaming about how I was going to spend my next fat paycheck.

About one hundred and fifty miles north, in the Catskill Mountain region, Dennis was also settling into a new job which he had just started the week before. He was the newly minted Activities Director at the Pines Hotel, a long-time staple of the borsch belt, in South Fallsburg, New York. He was in charge of coordinating the leisure activities for the Pines's guests, many of whom were from the geriatric crowd. The highlight of the entertainment was a spirited version of Simon Sez. Dennis remained upbeat and excited about the opportunity.

Dennis called me a few days before our birthday. He told me that he was having trouble with one of his co-workers, an old-timer who seemed threatened by Dennis's energy and enthusiasm. I told him to just be himself. He would soon win her over. Everybody loved Dennis. He had the good humor of a little boy and a sweet and generous temperament.

"Just keep working hard, pal," I offered. "She'll come around."

"I plan on it," he replied. Dennis proceeded to outline for me a series of radical changes to the activities program which he had conceived after an all-night brainstorming session. No stranger to the all-nighter myself, I thought nothing of it.

Dennis then told me that he supervised a crew of off-the-books workers who did all the labor such as rearranging chairs and the like. "Kev, you wouldn't believe it, but these guys work their butts off all day and get paid about ten dollars a day."

"Jesus," I cackled, "I make more than that when I'm taking a crap."

The voice on the other end of the phone went silent for a few seconds . . . then Dennis muttered something about needing to get back to work and ended the call. I regretted my crack immediately. I had offended Dennis's sense of dignity and pride. Ah, no big deal. I would straighten things out the next time I talked to him.

On the evening of October 20, 1990, I ordered Chinese food from a restaurant down the block and plopped myself on the couch to watch Game Four of the World Series between the Cincinnati Reds and Oakland A's. As is baseball's nature, the Series had broken exactly the opposite of how most of the experts had predicted. The A's had a fearsome lineup led by the Bash Brothers, Jose Canseco and Mark McGwire, long before the steroids scandal had diminished their legacies. In 1990 they were just sluggers; no one had a clue that their prodigious power strokes may have been enhanced artificially by the injection or ingestion of steroids. The notion of better baseball through chemistry had not yet crossed the cultural landscape.

The A's had won the Series in 1989 in a four game sweep over the San Francisco Giants, although the earthquake that hit right near the Oakland stadium just minutes before Game Three was scheduled to begin will be remembered long after any of the ballgames. The A's had also been in the Series in 1988 but lost to a vastly inferior L.A. Dodgers club which propelled itself to a championship on the back of a remarkably hot pitcher—Orel Hershiser—and a logic-defying game-winning homer by the hobbled Kirk Gibson off Dennis Eckersley in the bottom of the ninth of Game One.

1990 was supposed to be the year that the A's would cement themselves as an all-time great team. Instead, after losing the first three games to the Reds, who boasted an unparalleled trio of flame-throwing relievers: Randy Myers, Rob Dibble, and Norm Charlton, the A's were on the verge of going down as one of the all-time underachieving teams in baseball history. Although the Yankees did not smell the post-season that year, I had watched the Series with keen interest because the Reds were skippered by Lou Piniella, a boyhood hero, and I had encountered several of the Reds, specifically two of the aptly named Nasty Boys, at a bar in Pittsburgh in August.

Several of my college fraternity buddies—Pat Morris, Chuck Repsher, Keith Panza, and Erik Qualben—and I had embarked on a whirlwind two-week mid-America baseball tour in June, a few weeks after I had graduated from law school and several months before I would start my career as a corporate attorney in New York City.

I was a bit raw emotionally because the lovely young woman I had been dating in law school, Cindy Walker,[§] had shocked me with a late spring phone call in which she informed me out of the blue that she had accepted her hometown boyfriend's marriage proposal. Cindy had been honest with me from the start. I asked her out at least ten times before she agreed to go out with me. She kept saying no, she'd love to, but she had a boyfriend. I didn't care. I persisted until she said yes. After our first date, a movie, an electric jolt surged through my entire body when I kissed her while we stood at the end of the platform at the Ardmore train station. From then on, I couldn't get enough of her. She had brains, beauty, and a sweet heart. She never had broken up with this boyfriend but I had assumed, given the seemingly mutual intensity of our feelings for each other, that it was only a matter of time before Cindy would swing the hammer and end her earlier relationship. In the Spring of 1990, Cindy swung the proverbial hammer, but it hit me—not her hometown boyfriend—in the head and heart. But I was twenty-five, soon to be semi-rich, and fit as a fiddle. I had no doubt that this baseball trip with some of my best friends would yank me out of my blues.

We hit the games in a number of cities: Philadelphia, Pittsburgh, Chicago (Wrigley Field and Old Comiskey), Milwaukee and Cleveland, and then attacked the bars like men on a mission. In Pittsburgh we stormed a bar right next to Three Rivers Stadium after a Reds-Pirates game. I had zeroed in on a gorgeous brunette who was wearing a Mets cap—using the tried but true New York City connection wrap—and she agreed to dance with me. But as I gamely tried to perfect my robotic white man's shuffle and convince this lovely lass to make sweet music with me, she kept looking over my shoulder. Concerned that my dandruff had returned, I grew self-conscious and was almost relieved when I realized what she was looking for. Almost. It was Randy Myers. When she saw him she

[§] This is a pseudonym.

made a direct beeline—no excuse me, no thank you, no nothing—for him and he proceeded to give her a bear hug and kiss her for about three minutes without once coming up for air.

Norm Charlton, the third member of the Nasty Boys, had also sauntered into the bar. Still reeling from the Randy Myers-Mets chick cuckolding, I tried to make small talk with good old Norm.

"How you doing, Norm?" was my witty comment.

He looked at me for about half a second, just long enough for me to recognize that he had sized me up as about the equivalent value of excrement on his shoe, and snorted. Norm's guttural sniff, inarticulate as it was, spoke volumes about our respective pecking order in this sports bar. Here, where testosterone and athletic prowess were the only currencies that mattered, he—an ill-mannered rube from the sticks—was a king, and I—a recent law school graduate from the greatest city in the world—was a peon. I nevertheless was more bemused than resentful.

So the Nasty Boys liked the ladies more than a baseball fanatic from Brooklyn. Who could blame them? On this night in October, on my birthday, they were about to become World Champions.

Once again the Reds' pitching shut down the heralded A's lineup. They made it a clean sweep. In the first inning, though, Eric Davis, the Reds' star left fielder with a long and strong body built of muscle and sinew (he resembled a greyhound), had badly injured his kidney after diving for a line drive. He had to be removed from the field on a stretcher and taken by ambulance to a nearby hospital. As I watched the Reds celebrate, I felt enormous sympathy for Eric Davis. He had fulfilled his boyhood dream of winning a World Series but instead of being part of the celebration he was lying somewhere in a strange hospital being poked and prodded by doctors. What colossal unfairness. Even in victory the baseball gods can assert their will.

The A's manager, Tony LaRussa, trudged into his team's clubhouse amidst the Reds' raucous celebration. Highly regarded as a top manager, with an unused law degree as a frequently invoked testament to his supposed brilliance, LaRussa wore the shell-shocked look of a man who had just caught his wife *in flagrante delicto* with his best friend. On this night, there were no answers, no explanations. We watch the games, Tony, because the outcome is always in doubt. Because on this night, or on this day, we may see something that we have never seen before and will never see again. That is the inherent beauty of all sports, but only in baseball does complete surprise present itself as a regular guest.

It was well after midnight when I turned off the television. As I got ready to go to bed I realized that I had not heard from Dennis the entire day. It was the first time in our lives that we had not spoken to each other on our birthday. Even though we had attended different colleges in Pennsylvania and had lived apart since we were eighteen, we had always made it a point to contact each other on October 20th, wish ourselves a mutual happy birthday, and catch up a bit on our lives. Dennis did not have a telephone but he had previously always found a way to call me on our birthday. Not this day. Not this night. I did not think too much of this omission at the time. Dennis probably was too busy to find a phone. I would certainly hear from him in the next day or so. I thought everything was fine.

I could not possibly have been more wrong.

On the night of October 20, 1990, Dennis, after being fired from his job as Activities Director at the Pines Hotel, climbed out a second-floor window, jumped to the ground, and began running and crawling through the thick, dark woods that surrounded the hotel. He was convinced that he had stumbled upon a powerful international drug ring and that the bosses at the Pines—the leaders of the drug ring—were intent on murdering him because he had discovered too much, too soon.

After he exited the woods—a sneaker swallowed by the mud, his body, face and neck covered with scratches, cuts, and bruises—Dennis crawled to his car and began a panic-stricken drive to my mother's house in Manalapan, New Jersey. But, convinced that his would-be-murderers were tailing him, he pulled off the Garden State Parkway at Exit 154 and headed to the Clifton, New Jersey Police Station. Once inside the station, after Dennis called my father, he became convinced—when, in his view, my dad took too long to arrive at the station—that my father was part of the Pines's drug ring and, too, was intent on killing him.

When the police officers told him he was free to go, Dennis became terrified, convinced that his life was in grave danger if he left the safety of the police station. So, to ensure that he would not be discharged, Dennis made a half-hearted effort to grab a gun from one of the officer's holster. Dennis was lucky that he was not shot dead on the spot.

The cops at the station threw Dennis to the ground, restrained him in a strait-jacket, and eventually sent him to a local psychiatric hospital for evaluation. At that time, only my father, a seasoned cop, could fathom that my brother had lost his sanity, his grip on reality. Sean and I, who, after receiving frantic phone calls from my mom, had raced to the Clifton Police Station to see Dennis, actually considered and, for a short while, credited, Dennis's fanciful claims about the Pines's drug ring. We did not realize that Dennis was insane until he insisted to us in a paranoid whisper that my father was part of the international drug ring and that my dad, too, was trying to murder him. Sean and I both realized immediately that my father, who loved all five of his children dearly, would never try to intentionally hurt, let alone kill, any of us.

Over the next few years, Dennis alternated between fighting to regain his sanity and reveling in his Messianic delusions which led him to believe, at various times, that he was John the Baptist, Jesus Christ, or God the Father.[6] During the times that he believed that he was God of one iteration or another, Dennis was confident that the physical laws of the universe did not apply to him. He would, for instance, frequently cross the busy Gordon Corners Road intersection in Manalapan with his head down, oblivious and—in his mind—impervious, to the scores of cars that whizzed past him in both directions.

During this time, my family struggled to help Dennis regain his bearings, to find his true, sane self, and to find some measure of happiness amidst the flood of psychotic thoughts that infected his brain. For me, it was beyond discomfiting to see my beloved twin brother embrace with his whole being the notion that he was not a mere mortal, not just a man, but God Almighty in the flesh. But, in a strange irony, Dennis was much happier when he believed that he was God. My twin believed that it was far better to be a deity—the ruler of the universe, no less—than a heavily medicated mental patient with no ability to function in or fit into the community.

CHAPTER NINETEEN

Heart of Stone

They say a good love is one that sits you down, gives you a drink of wa-
ter, and pats you on top of the head. But I say a good love is one that casts
you into the wind, sets you ablaze, makes you burn through the skies and
ignite the night like a phoenix; the kind that cuts you loose like a wildfire
and you can't stop running simply because you keep on burning every-
thing that you touch! I say that's a good love; one that burns and flies, and
you run with it!

— C. JoyBell C.

In early November 1990, just a few weeks after Dennis's mental break-down, I heard a soft knock at my apartment door as I laid sprawled on the couch, alone, watching a college football game. When I opened the door I was startled to see the pretty yet solemn face of Cindy Walker.

"What the hell are you doing here?" I blurted.

"I really need to talk to you. It's important," she said.

I invited Cindy in, took her coat, and beckoned her to sit on my sofa. Cindy was wearing a short black skirt and a white, sleeveless, silk blouse. She was a picture of beauty and grace.

"I need to talk to you. And I need you to listen. Can you promise me you'll let me finish before you say anything?"

"OK," I mumbled.

"OK, then. I realize I've made a big mistake. When Pete asked me to marry him, I felt like I didn't have any choice. I love him ... very much, in fact, but I'm not in love with him. I'm in love with you. When I'm with him, I'm with him for him. But when I'm with you, I'm with you for me. I realize this now. I know it for sure. I love you, Kevin. I'm in love with you. I want to be with you. Only you. Starting right now."

Cindy stopped talking and brushed away her dirty blonde hair from her face. Her beautiful hazel eyes, moist and red, looked deeply into mine, beseeching me, begging me, say something you big lug. Tell me you love me too.

If I could have stopped that moment in time and reflected on what was happening, I would have soon realized that this was a watershed moment, not just in Cindy's life, but mine as well. This young and beautiful woman, blessed with kindness, tenderness, intelligence, ambition, and a quirky sense of humor—which mirrored my oddball view of things— was proposing to me. She was telling me that she wanted to marry me, wanted to spend the rest of her life with me, wanted to have my children, and wanted to grow old with me. This woman, laid bare, raw and vulnerable, fully exposed, emotionally naked, deserved at minimum my respect and tenderness.

She received neither. After I told her what had happened to Dennis over the last few weeks, I told her, bluntly and unequivocally, that I was in no condition to begin a relationship with her or anyone else. My heart, for some reason, had turned to marble. I felt no love for her, only anger and resentment that she had chosen the hometown boyfriend over me.

I talked to her and treated her with no grace, no chivalry, no gentility. I treated this woman, who professed her sincere and profound love for me, as badly, callously, and cruelly as a man could treat a woman.

And it was not just my brother's descent into mental illness that calcified my heart. That explanation is too easy, an excuse, a crutch, not an answer. The cold, hard truth is that at the time I lacked the emotional maturity, the strength of character, really, to both accept and return the love offered to me by Cindy.

An hour or so after Cindy entered my apartment, we left together. I haled a cab and climbed in after Cindy, careful to keep my hands at my sides, lest she get the idea that I had changed my mind. We arrived at Penn Station to await the train that would take Cindy back to Philadelphia. We sat on one of the upstairs benches, side by side, neither uttering a word. Her tears flowed freely; my face remained a stone. The forty-five minutes we waited for her train to arrive at the station seemed like a month.

The station announcer called out that Cindy's train had arrived. Cindy stopped crying and shot me a hard glare.

"Why are you being such an asshole?"

I had no answer and just lowered my head in surrender. She burst into sobs and headed for the stairs which would take her to her train to Philadelphia and out of my life forever. Still sobbing, once on the stairs, she turned her head back toward me. Not once, not twice, but three times. Each time I looked away, not daring to lock eyes.

'Til the end, she hoped that I would have a last second change of heart and give her a storybook ending. True love meets true love. And all is right with the world. But I was not the man she thought I was. Hell, I was not even the man I thought I was. On this night, one long ago November Saturday, I was destined to disappoint. And not just Cindy.

When Cindy finally disappeared into the dark tunnel of Penn Station, I knew that I had just committed an atrocity. I turned my back on love. On a person who loved me deeply. Who was damn easy to love herself. I rewarded Cindy's brave and meaningful declaration of love with a quick, bitter, and malicious slap of rejection.

I took the coward's way out. Heart of stone. No need to love anyone else. No room to feel strongly about another person. I had all I could do to maintain the peace and harmony of my own circle of love. No need to widen the circle. It was just too much trouble; not worth the pain and aggravation.

Karma, truly ... ain't she a bitch.

CHAPTER TWENTY

The Edge

When the body sinks into death, the essence of man is revealed. Man is a knot, a web, a mesh into which relationships are tied. Only those relationships matter. The body is an old crock that nobody will miss. I have never known a man to think of himself when dying. Never.

— Antoine De Saint-Exupery

On August 23, 1993, I spent the day in the New York Public Library, flanked by imposing white marble lions on both sides of the matching white marble stairs, and researched the possibility of initiating a Civil RICO lawsuit against various politicians and political contributors for blatant violations of campaign finance laws through the ubiquitous practice of "bundling," in which individuals or entities group small contributions together to evade financial contribution donation limits.

Say, for instance, that I, Mr. Moneybags, owner of a mid-sized investment bank, want to donate a million dollars to a candidate for the United States Senate but am constrained by the campaign finance law in my state which limits the amount of any single contribution to $100,000.00. I can circumvent this cap by soliciting, on a tacit pay or your fired basis, $5,000.00 each from my bank's two hundred employees. After I collect all two hundred checks, I present them in a bundled million dollar package to the candidate, Mr. Sellhissoul Forelection, as a gift from "Mr. Moneybags and friends."

Mr. Sellhissoul Forelection will then no doubt pay me back with favorable regulatory rulings, bond issuances, or governmental appointments, once he assumes his seat in the cradle of democracy.

The Racketeering, Influence & Corruption Act ("RICO") was enacted by Congress in 1970 as a legal mechanism to punish mobsters who were engaging in conspiracies to commit crimes. The idea was to ensnare the Mafia don who gave the order but didn't pull the trigger and punish him for the crimes that were the subject of the conspiracy. The drafters of RICO included a civil provision which allows litigants to sue for treble (triple) damages to their "business and property" which were caused by RICO violations.

Within a few years, numerous creative lawyers were dreaming up new applications of Civil RICO, which became known as the "nuclear bomb" of litigation, that were far afield from the scope contemplated by the statute's drafters. In short order, though, the federal courts began to rein in many of these litigation excesses and construed many of the pleading elements for RICO cases strictly. Consequently, given all the procedural roadblocks, it became rare for a RICO case to survive a motion to dismiss at the threshold pleading stage.

This was the issue which obsessed me on August 23, 1993. I was convinced that the proper application of RICO, in the right case and with the right judge, could diminish substantially, if not destroy, the pernicious, anti-democratic practice of "bundling." I had my precedent cases in related areas and had begun to structure my soon to be ground-breaking complaint. Now all I needed to do was to find someone to serve as a plaintiff in the case and to pick the right forum.

That afternoon, my mother, sister, and brother, Sean, were visiting my brother Dennis at his workplace, Tony Roma's, a Broadway rib joint, before viewing an early evening performance of *Les Miserables*. It was a family reunion of sorts but when I sauntered in with my briefcase full of

RICO-related notes and cases, I could tell by my mother's worried look that something was wrong.

"It's Dennis," she told me in a hushed voice. "He's manic. We think he's sick again."

Dennis had been working at Tony Roma's as an assistant manager for about a month. It was his first job since his mental breakdown on October 20, 1990. In retrospect, his fragile psyche was probably made more vulnerable by the erratic hours he worked and the hustle and bustle of Broadway.

I could tell Dennis had had a relapse the moment I saw him. His eyes were glassy. His body was in New York but his mind was some place far away. He introduced me to his co-workers. "Guys, this is my twin brother, Kevin. And let me tell you something, he is a great, and I mean great, lawyer . . . the greatest, in fact."

This overblown praise for my legal skills went on all night. To hear Dennis tell it, I was a cross between Clarence Darrow and F. Lee Bailey. At the time, I was unemployed with but an idea—albeit a provocative and interesting one—in my legal portfolio. I thus deflected all praise with as much true modesty as I could muster.

When Dennis came home from work late that evening, I talked to him for more than an hour. I knew that I needed to drag him to the hospital the next day for a new round of examinations, diagnoses, and prescribed medications, and I knew that he would resist every part of this process with all his strength (which was considerably greater than mine).

I told Dennis that I too had walked the edge and that I knew how it felt to straddle the fine line between insanity and genius and inspiration. But I really didn't and he knew that I was a false prophet.

I told him that we needed to go to the hospital in the morning and he agreed to that without complaint. His quick assent should have been enough to signal to me that Dennis had no intention of being dragged into a mental hospital for a psychiatric work-up, but I was tired and stressed, and I heard what I wanted to hear. Maybe this time it was not going to be as bad as I thought.

At the end of our talk, Dennis's eyes cleared for a moment. He looked at me, as sane as ever, placed his hand gently on my cheek, and said, "Kevin, I know you love me."

Those were the last words I ever heard my brother speak.

CHAPTER TWENTY-ONE

Kiss of Death

It was written I should be loyal to the nightmare of my choice.

— Joseph Conrad, *Heart of Darkness*

O n the morning of August 24, 1993, I woke up two hours late, at about 9:00 a.m., in my apartment on Boulevard East in Wee-hawken, New Jersey, which I shared with my brothers, Dennis and Sean, and Sean's girlfriend, Starlight—a beautiful, exotic brunette, who was trying to make it in New York City as a singer. Sean and Starlight had both left for work. I headed to the office at the front of our apartment, which faced Boulevard East and provided a beautiful view of the New York skyline. Dennis, who slept on a light foam mattress in the office, was nowhere to be found. A folded up copy of the *New York Times* had been left atop his mattress, but everything else seemed in place and in order.

Damn, I thought. He knows I had planned to take him to a New York City hospital for a psychiatric work-up. His consent last night had been a ruse, a ploy to buy some time, to get me off his back until he could figure out what to do. And his thoughts, his plan, were no doubt irrational, fueled by delusions of his divinity or anything else that popped into his creative yet diseased brain.

I showered quickly and took a min-van bus to the Port Authority in New York City. I walked into Tony Roma's at East 44th or 45th Street and Broadway, and asked the manager if he had seen Dennis. He told me that Dennis had been scheduled to work at 9:00 a.m. but had neither shown up nor called in. When I heard that information, my stomach turned queasy. Dennis could be anywhere and could be doing anything. Dennis, on the loose, with money in his pockets, was a dangerous man—mostly to himself.

I started to walk up 42nd Street and passed Bryant Park and the New York Public Library (on 5th Avenue). I was looking for Dennis but realized that I was looking for the proverbial needle in a haystack. It was, after all, a big city.

I started to think about Dennis and his battle with mental illness. The doctors had diagnosed him as a schizophrenic but Dennis hated that label, and his particular psychosis did not fit easily into any schizophrenic category, so I tried to avoid using that word whenever possible.

After his initial breakdown on October 20, 1990, our twenty-sixth birthday, when Dennis became terrified that his former bosses at the Pines Hotel (and then, later, my father) were trying to kill him, Dennis had never exhibited any traces of paranoia. As soon as he came to live within the comfort of my mother's home, he was no longer in fear of his life. But his mental illness had the devastating impact of convincing Dennis, from time to time, that certain members of his nuclear family were evil and his enemies.

Dennis initially thought that my father was out to kill him because he arrived—in Dennis's view—late to the Clifton, New Jersey Police Station on the morning of October 21, 1990. Several months later, when the glass frame of a family photograph fell to the ground—and the glass cracked parallel to my sister Deirdre's head, Dennis was sure that Deirdre was Satan's messenger.

Then, inexplicably, one night my loving mother became—in Dennis's sick mind—his mortal enemy. That night, after Dennis gave my mother the "kiss of death," mimicking Michael Corleone's kiss of his brother Fredo—with both hands planted firmly on the sides of her head before a hard, quick kiss on the mouth—the poor woman went to bed with several butcher's knives under her bed. It was almost inconceivable that Dennis, an extraordinarily loving and gentle son, could make his own mother fear for her life, but that is what happened.

And even I, Dennis's twin, was not immune from his psychotic delusions. At one point, Dennis, convinced that he was God, the perfect being, pure love incarnate, became convinced that I must be his opposite: Satan, Lucifer, evil in the flesh. It was early autumn, cool but not cold, with the leaves just starting to fall to the ground, when Dennis asked if I would have a catch with him. I quickly agreed, and asked him if he knew where my glove was.

"It's OK, Kev," he said. "You won't need a glove. I just want to soft toss."

Dennis and I stood on the lawn in front of my mom's house and started to lob a baseball back and forth to each other. His throws were soft but labored. He bounced quite a few and asked me to come closer. I moved in a few feet. He bounced a few more throws.

"Closer," he said, as he waved me toward him with his right arm.

I complied and stood a mere twenty feet or so from Dennis.

"That's good," he said.

He then started to throw considerably harder. One throw stung my bare hand.

"Take it easy," I said.

"OK, just one more."

Dennis took two steps closer to me and flipped the ball into the air with his right hand. When he caught it, he took a crow-hop, reared back, and threw the ball as hard as he could right at my head. At the last split second, I tilted my head back and heard the ball as it whizzed past my left ear. The baseball ricocheted off the edge of my mother's house and into her neighbors' yard.

"What the hell was that?" I screamed at my brother.

Dennis looked at me and flashed a lopsided grin. He felt no remorse. He had actually tried to hit me, to hurt me, with the baseball. And he came just a few inches away from succeeding.

Such was the power of Dennis's mental illness. It took the Dennis that we knew and loved and turned him into someone else entirely. As I searched in vain for Dennis that late August day, I fretted about the final manifestation of Dennis's mental illness. I prayed that Dennis—an exceptionally strong man—would not hurt, or, worse, kill someone he loved while in the grip of his delusions. If that were ever to happen, if Dennis were to escape from his delusional state and regain his sanity, he would be inconsolable, devastated beyond description.

By early afternoon, I was tired and frustrated. I stopped for a cheeseburger at Hamburger Heaven on East 49th Street. As I devoured my juicy, delicious burger, I realized that I was looking for Dennis in the wrong city.

A few nights earlier, while we were watching a Yankees game in the living room of our apartment, my brothers and I were talking about the death of Vincent Foster, the White House lawyer who turned up dead of a gunshot wound to the mouth at Fort Marcy Park (in McLean, Virginia) on July 20, 1993.

The initial reports indicated that Foster had become severely depressed over numerous problems in connection with his job—providing a myriad of legal services for President Bill Clinton and his wife, Hillary (Foster's former law partner). I told Sean and Dennis that it didn't make sense to me that Vince Foster had killed himself.

"I don't know, guys, it just smells to me. This guy had too much to live for to let some work nonsense make him want to end it all. I don't know what happened but the cover story just seems like bullshit to me."

Dennis walked back into the office and emerged with a recent *New York Times* article that reported that there was no reasonable doubt:

Vince Foster had committed suicide. He flipped the newspaper to me. I flipped it back to him without reading the article on Foster's death.

"Just because the *New York Times* prints something doesn't make it true, Dennis," I said.

"I just read in a JFK book that a few weeks after the assassination the *New York Times* printed a lengthy article which made a compelling, no doubt about it case that Lee Harvey Oswald was the lone gunman in Dallas. And you know that that story was a fairytale."

"So who do you think murdered Vince Foster?" Dennis asked.

"Listen, Dennis. I'm not saying that he was murdered. I'm not saying that he killed himself. I'm saying that I don't know what happened. And that someone should do a thorough investigation. That's all I'm saying."

Days later, as I sat in a booth at Hamburger Heaven, I deduced that Dennis had gone to Washington, D.C. to conduct an investigation, his investigation, into the death of Vincent Foster. I paid my bill and hurried home to my Weehawken apartment.

When I arrived back at our apartment, I entered the office and checked the copy of the *New York Times* that was lying atop Dennis's mattress. Sure enough it was turned open to the article that concluded that Vince Foster had committed suicide. Period. End of story.

Dennis had left that paper on his bed as a clue for me. He no doubt intended for me to follow him. I started to pack a duffel bag for my imminent trip to Washington, D.C. I hoped that I could intercept Dennis before he did anything stupid, before he got hurt. Just as I was about to head out the door my phone rang.

I picked up the receiver and heard my mother's gentle voice.

"Kevin, you need to sit down," she said.

"I don't want to sit down, Mom," I said. "Tell me what happened."

"Dennis is gone, Kevin, he's gone. He drowned in Baltimore a few hours ago."

My mother proceeded to tell me the rest of the story. Dennis had purchased a one way Greyhound bus ticket to Washington, D.C. (just as

I suspected). When the bus stopped in Baltimore, Dennis exited and walked a short distance to the Korean War Memorial, across from the Baltimore Harbor, and just around the corner from Camden Yards (home of the Baltimore Orioles). Two twelve-year-old boys were having a catch with a pink, rubber, spaldeen ball. An errant throw sailed into the harbor. Dennis jumped into the Baltimore Harbor to retrieve the spaldeen. But he could not swim. So he drowned, flailing in desperation, reaching for that pink spaldeen, crying out for help, in full view of several dozen people who watched the tragedy unfold from the safe (and dry) confines of the Korean War Memorial.

While I was still on the phone with my mother, Sean and Starlight walked into the apartment. The look of horror on my face told them that something awful had happened. I hung up the phone and told them that Dennis had died. Sean, Starlight, and I hugged each other as hard as we could stand it.

A little more than an hour later, we picked up my brother Thomas at the Port Authority in New York City. Thomas was an architecture student at Catholic University in Washington, D.C. As he prepared to return to college for his sophomore year, Thomas was staying for a few days at my dad and Willie's Rockland County apartment. But Thomas was alone in their apartment that day, as my dad and Willie had driven to the Garden State Arts Center (in Holmdel, New Jersey) for an Anne Murray concert. After my mother had called my dad's home, and conveyed the awful news to my youngest brother, Thomas had quickly hopped on a bus to New York City.

After we picked up Thomas, we drove to my mother's house in Manalapan. There was an eery silence in the car as Sean, Starlight, Thomas, and I headed south to my mother's home. None of us could give voice to his or her feelings.

When we arrived in Manalapan, each of us—Mom, Sean, Deirdre, Thomas, Starlight, and I—alternated between stoic composure and hysterical crying jags. But we were all there for each other and comforted each other as best as we could.

But my father was not there. We decided that I needed to be the one to tell my dad that his second oldest son had died. My father, on summer evenings, was almost always in his easy chair watching the Yankees. But, on this night, his phone kept ringing and ringing, as my dad and Willie had still not returned from the concert in New Jersey.

At 10:00 p.m. or so, finally, seated in my mom's kitchen booth, sandwiched between Joe and Kristian Gregorace—father and son, and family friends, who were at my mom's house for emotional support—I called my dad's number and Willie picked up the phone. I told her that Dennis had drowned that afternoon.

She whispered to me, "Kevin, your father has a bad heart. I don't want him to die."

"I know, Willie. I don't want him to die either, but I need to tell him what happened."

My father—probably worried already by Thomas's unexpected departure—must have seen the stricken look in Willie's eyes.

"What's going on!" he shouted. "Give me the damn phone!"

I heard his booming voice. "Kevin, what happened? What's going on?"

I told my father, as dispassionately as possible, that Dennis had died.

"No, no, no!" my father cried.

Joe and Kristian squeezed into my shoulders at both ends of the booth. They were literally and figuratively providing me with support, with an anchor.

I then recounted for my father the prior evening, when Dennis had turned manic, when his eyes had turned to glass, when he had readily agreed to let me take him to a hospital for a psychiatric work-up.

"Jesus Christ, Kevin, how the hell could you have let him leave the apartment?" my dad wailed.

"He got up early, Dad," I said. "He was gone before I got up. What the hell should I have done? Chained him to the bed?"

"I'm coming over. I'll be there as soon as I can," my dad said, and he hung up the phone.

Less than two hours later, my father and Willie pulled into my mom's driveway. My father, always neat, well-groomed, and clean shaven, looked a mess. He had problems putting in his false teeth, his dentures, so he left them home. He arrived toothless, disheveled, and emotionally devastated.

He and Willie stayed for several hours. His presence was comforting to all of his children and even—at least a little bit—to my mom, despite the bad blood that had been shed in their still fresh divorce.

An hour or two after midnight, as my dad and Willie were getting ready to drive back to their home in Rockland County, my father hugged and kissed each of his children goodbye. When he stood before me, the last child to talk to him that night, I looked him in the eyes, stuck out my right hand, and said, stiffly and formally, as if I were addressing a stranger, "thanks for coming, tonight, Dad. We appreciate it."

He looked at me like a wounded deer, grabbed my right arm, pulled me in for a tight hug, and whispered in my ear.

"Thanks for coming? Really? Where the hell do you think I would go? You guys are my family. You're everything to me."

When my father left, we were all physically and emotionally exhausted. After everyone else went to bed, my mother, with incredible strength and grace, continued to comfort me. She then told me that I should sleep in Dennis's old bedroom.

After I kissed my mom goodnight, I went to that bedroom and looked out the window into her backyard.

A heavy rain had begun to crash to the ground. Soon thunder began to roar, at first far away, then louder, closer, more frequently. And the lightning followed: sharp bursts of light that flashed through the black sky like violent thrusts into a defenseless torso. The thunder grew even louder. It rattled the house.

I remembered that as children Dennis and I were both terrified of thunder. One time, my mother or father—I don't remember which one— tried to allay our fear.

"It's OK, guys. Thunder can't hurt you. Think of it like as if God is bowling."

As the thunder continued to roar with anger, I tried to spin it into a positive context: God was celebrating the arrival of Dennis. He was welcoming my brother into his kingdom with loud applause and hoopla.

But that image, that notion, faded quickly. This thunder, this lightning, was funereal, not celebratory. It was a requiem, a dirge, not an anthem. The world had tilted off its axis. The universe was out of alignment. My brother, Dennis, a bright, shining light, was no more. And so was the infant, the toddler, the boy, the man, the twin, that I had been for twenty-eight years.

CHAPTER TWENTY-TWO

The Bostonians

To the living we owe respect, but to the dead we owe only the truth.

— Voltaire

The day after Dennis died, Sean and I were at my mom's home when her phone rang. Sean picked it up. The funeral director was preparing Dennis's body for his wake and needed us to bring the clothes in which Dennis would be buried to the funeral home. Sean and I set about performing this grim task.

We picked out Dennis's favorite gray flannel suit and, if I remember correctly, a crisp white shirt and bright red pattern tie. So far so good. But we hit a roadblock when it came to footwear. Dennis did not have a single pair of shoes in my mother's house.

Sean had a brainstorm and reached into the brown paper bag which contained the clothes Dennis wore when he had drowned: a T-shirt, jeans, briefs, white socks, and sneakers. He pulled out the sneakers: white with blue stripes on the sides.

"Maybe we can use these," Sean said. "The casket is going to be closed. No one will even notice."

I grabbed the sneakers, examined them, and shook my head. These sneakers, no longer soggy, but cracked and stiff from their plunge into the Baltimore Harbor, would not be placed on Dennis's feet for all eternity. That would not do. No one else would know. But we would know.

I walked to the closet in my bedroom at my mom's house, reached down, and picked up a shoe box. I had recently purchased a brand new pair of black leather shoes, Bostonians, wing-tip loafers, with tassels in the front. I had planned to unveil these shoes for my upcoming job interviews. But fate had intervened. Fate had another plan for these Bostonians.

I opened the box, picked up the new shoes, and placed them in the plastic bag in which we had packed Dennis's belt, socks, underwear, and tie. (Sean had placed the shirt and suit on a wooden hanger).

"We're good, Sean. Found a pair of shoes. You're good to go."

Sean nodded. One less thing to worry about. He threw the hanger over his right shoulder, grabbed the plastic bag with his left hand, and headed for his car.

Alone in my mother's house, I contemplated for about the hundredth time whether I wanted to view my twin brother's body. A part of me longed to do so, to say goodbye, to touch gently his cheek and wish him peace. But I was leaning strongly against a viewing. Dennis was an affirmation of life. He was constant motion. He was alive, always so alive, just about the most alive person I had ever known.

I did not want my last memory of Dennis to be a look at his inert corpse. I feared that such an image would be everlasting and, eventually, would swallow up all my other memories of Dennis so that every time I thought of him all I would be able to see would be his lifeless shell lying in a box, in a gray suit and red tie.

Maybe a part of me, also, did not want to see my mirror reflection in a dead body. Dennis was gone. I was all that was left of our twin kingdom. Maybe I just couldn't bear the thought of being the sole surviving standard-bearer. The only twin left who could fulfill his dreams on this earth. The yin without the yang.

It was all quite too much too handle. I decided that I would not see Dennis's body. I had already seen Dennis for the last time. And he had told me that he knew that I loved him. And I knew with metaphysical certainty that he felt the same way about me.

That was all it, all we, could ever be. We had come to the end of the line.

Would it be enough?

CHAPTER TWENTY-THREE

The Tide

Death is not an event in life: we do not live to experience death. If we take eternity to mean not infinite temporal duration but timelessness, then eternal life belongs to those who live in the present.

— Ludwig Wittgenstein

Near the end of his long and accomplished life, Carl Jung, a preeminent 20th century psychiatrist and psychotherapist, wrote about the possibility of life after death.

He noted that "[p]arapsychology holds it to be a scientifically valid proof of an afterlife that the dead manifest themselves—either as ghosts, or through a medium—and communicate things which they alone could possibly know." [7]

But in the next breath, Jung emphasized that even though many well-documented cases of presumably post-death communications exist, "the question remains whether the ghost or the voice is identical with the dead person or is a psychic projection, and whether the things said really derive from the deceased or from knowledge which may be present in the unconscious." [8]

Talking ghosts or unconscious knowledge? That question, as posed, can never be answered satisfactorily because it is an existential chicken or egg riddle. But Carl Jung was not afraid to recount his own life ex-

137

periences to at least shed light on his considered opinion as to whether the dead can communicate with the living.

Jung recounted an evening where he laid awake in deep thought about the unexpected death of a friend whose funeral he had attended the day before. After sensing his friend's presence in the room, Jung had to convince himself that the inner visual image of his friend that he perceived was real rather than a fantasy. When Jung decided to give his friend the benefit of the doubt and credit his reality, his friend went to the door and motioned Jung to follow him.[9]

He led me out of the house, into the garden, out to the road, and finally to his house ... I went in, and he conducted me to his study. He climbed on a stool and showed me the second of five books with red bindings which stood on the second shelf from the top. Then the vision broke off. I was not acquainted with his library and did not know what books he owned ...

[The] next morning I went to his widow and asked whether I could look up something in my friend's library. Sure enough, there was a stool standing under the bookcase I had seen in my vision, and even before I came closer I could see the five books with red bindings. I stepped up on the stool as to be able to read the titles. They were translations of the novels of Emile Zola. The title of the second volume read: "The Legacy of the Dead." The contents seemed to me of no interest. Only the title was extremely significant in connection with this experience.[10]

The night Dennis died, his voice came to my mother in a dream. "Page 346 mom, page 346," she heard my brother say. Startled, she woke up immediately, and believed that Dennis had referred to his transcript, *Grand Delusions*, a detailed journal of his two-and-a-half year battle with mental illness.

My mother had not yet read *Grand Delusions*, so the number 346 meant nothing to her. But she complied with Dennis's instructions, turned on the lights, went into Dennis's room, and pulled the typed manuscript out of his dresser drawer. She turned to page 346. In the middle of that page, seemingly incongruent to and out of context with the point Dennis was trying to make in his book, stood these words: *"The battle was over and we had won! It had been a particularly bloody battle, but the power of love could not be defeated. Thank you all for fighting with me. The war is not over yet, but it won't be long now. Tonight we have irreversibly turned the tide."* [11]

My mother took great comfort in these words. She, a woman of strong Catholic faith, believed that Dennis had sent her a message to let her and the rest of my family know that he was all right. And that the death of his body had not extinguished the extraordinary power of his love. From that moment, secure in her belief that Dennis's soul was still very much alive, my mother was at peace over the loss of her son.

As for me, I was heartened that my mother had found something to grasp onto to ease her pain but I did not take much stock in her perceived paranormal experience. In all my glorious egocentrism, I figured for sure that if Dennis were inclined to communicate with someone from beyond the grave, he would have chosen me, his twin, to receive his message.

For years I waited for Dennis to make contact with me. I expected him to appear before me in a vision, or at least a dream, when I needed him the most. But Dennis did not make his presence known to me in any manifestation. He was gone. Simply gone. And for a long time, quite a long time, I was lost.

CHAPTER TWENTY-FOUR

Suicide Squeeze

To try is to risk failure, but risks must be taken, because the greatest hazard in life is to risk nothing.

— Leo Buscaglia, *Living, Loving, and Learning*

M y father loved to have our Cadets sandlot teams bunt. He constantly drilled us in bunting fundamentals: square all the way around, catch the ball with your bat—don't stab at it, keep the bathead lower than your shoulders, hold the bat like you're holding a pen—don't wrap those fingers around the barrel—that's how you'll break 'em, tilt the barrel toward the lines—keep that ball away from the pitcher.

He made sure that every one of his players could bunt competently. If you could not bunt in batting practice, you didn't get a chance to hit. No good bunts, no swings. So everyone learned how to bunt.

I remember a game at Erasmus Hall High School (my grandfather's alma mater) when I was about twelve. My father had five batters in a row lay down bunts. All reached safely. The opposing coach become livid.

"Can't your guys hit the damn ball? What's with this Mickey Mouse garbage?"

141

"Teach your kids how to make the play, and I'll have them hit away," my father replied.

But he relented and had me, the sixth batter, hit away. I hit a grand slam to left field. As I rounded third, the opposing coach slammed his hat to the ground. My father just laughed.

My dad's favorite play—without question—was the suicide squeeze. It is the most daring of plays and can only be used with less than two outs and a runner on third base. The key to the play is that the runner breaks for home just a split second before the pitch is about to be released. He must wait for the pitcher to have begun his throw home, for if the pitcher sees the runner breaking mid-delivery, he can make a last-second adjustment and throw the ball high and tight, forcing the batter to hit the dirt, or high and away, preventing the batter from reaching the pitch. Either way, if the batter misses the bunt, the catcher usually has the ball in his glove and can easily tag out the runner before he touches home plate.

A lot of things must go right for this play to work. First and fore-most, the batter and the runner must be on the same wavelength. If the runner thinks the squeeze is on but the batter misses the sign, the runner is in serious danger of being struck by a foul ball or the hitter's bat as he swings it through the zone. To combat this risk, the batter needs to give the runner an acknowledgement that he has received the squeeze sign and knows the play is on. My father used to have the batter take off his helmet to acknowledge the play. At higher levels, the signal can be more discreet, but there always must be a batter acknowledgement.

The benefit of the play is that if it is executed well it is a near certain run. All the batter needs to do is put the bunt down on the ground in fair territory. With the runner barreling toward home, if the bunt hits the ground the runner will almost always be safe at home.

The Yankees, especially under their last two managers, Joe Torre and Joe Girardi, have almost never used the suicide squeeze. Torre's reluctance to put on the squeeze was to my father's jaded view proof positive of some serious character defect, notwithstanding that my dad and Joe Torre had been friends, classmates, and baseball teammates at St. Francis Prep (which was then located in Brooklyn) in the late 1950s.

My father used to go nuts every time the Yankees stranded a runner on third in the late innings. "This is the perfect time for a squeeze," Dad would say. Two outs later, when the Yanks failed to score a run they needed desperately, he'd mutter, "Should've tried the squeeze. Have some imagination. Find a way to manufacture some damn runs."

I must have heard a version of this song several dozen times. The suicide squeeze appealed to my father's taste for risk and his love of gambling. When it worked, when the bunt hit the ground, and the runner soon thereafter stepped triumphantly on home plate, my father beamed. And when it failed, when the batter missed the bunt and the runner was hung out to dry, my father could handle it. He would place his hands at his sides, with his palms facing upwards toward the sky, as if to say, Damn, I taught that kid how to bunt. I can't believe he missed that pitch.

The bottom line on the suicide squeeze was that my father, far more than most men, was not afraid to fail. He was not content to always make the safe play. Not by a long shot.

One final thought on the suicide squeeze: when you think about it, the name is a terrible misnomer. There is nothing "suicidal" about a team that tries a suicide squeeze. It is not trying to have its runner thrown out at home. It realizes that the runner will be "dead" if the play fails, but its intent is the exact opposite: the runner should be safe, alive.

A more appropriate name for the play, if we want to stay in the negative, is we-know-we-are-dead-if-this-play-fails-squeeze. If using a positive context, we could call it the runner-will-be-safe-as-long-as-the-batter-lays-down-a-halfway-decent-bunt-squeeze.

But this is all semantics. We all know that this play—rare as it is nowadays—will always be called the "suicide squeeze." It matters not a whit that this label, this description, could not be more inaccurate. That's the name of the play and we are stuck with it.

CHAPTER TWENTY-FIVE

Occam's Razor

With him, life was routine; without him, life was unbearable.

— Harper Lee, *To Kill a Mockingbird*

In the Summer of 1994 I was in hell. For starters, at the end of July, the exalted leaders of Major League Baseball and the Major League Baseball Players Association thought it prudent to shut down the game. Unable to reach a compromise as to how to divide the untold millions of dollars earned by baseball, the owners had the audacity to tell the players to take their balls and bats and go home. Just as brazenly, and foolishly, the players complied and went on strike. For the first time in more than one hundred years, through several world wars and a few other major military conflicts, there would be no World Series played in October. To compound the indignity, at the time the players went on strike the New York Yankees were in first place in the American League East Division and looked for the first time in quite a while as the team to beat in the American League. But in 1994 the Major League Baseball strike was the least of my problems.

I had exiled myself to Philadelphia, a National League town with an inferiority complex. I was working with two of my classmates from Villanova Law School, Allen Tucci and Michael Semes, who had opened their own law firm on Chestnut Street, in the heart of Philadelphia's famously aggressive legal community. Like me, Allen and Mike had graduated from Villanova Law School just four years earlier; unlike me, they had already acquired some major clients, including a fast-rising minority-owned bank. Allen and Mike specialized in banking and regulatory work, which was not my area of expertise. They had several other attorneys working for them, but agreed to take me on to try and develop a litigation department for the firm. The only catch was that I would not receive a straight salary; I would be paid a percentage of the litigation bills sent and received by the firm for my services. The percentage was quite fair, but the deal anticipated that I would solicit my own clients and my own cases for the firm. The job was entirely what I made it.

In theory at least, the law is about a search for justice. Justice, a blunt word for fundamental fairness, is the goal for every lawyer who ever laced up his wingtips. I demand justice for my client. Justice system. (David Justice ... sorry, I digress). Justice. The word rolls off the tongue easily, and has a noble, almost self-righteous, quality. There are far worse things to do with your life than to strive to use all your skills and determination to carve out some real justice in your corner of the world, whether in the streets of Flatbush Avenue in Brooklyn or the hallowed courtrooms of Philadelphia. But to fight for justice you have to have some belief in your heart that justice is possible.

In 1994 my belief in justice was dead and buried with my brother. I viewed the world and its inhabitants through an incessant prism of injustice. I would go to a bar, see some guy laughing at something stupid and think: what an asshole, this guy has no right to breathe, let alone laugh; he can't even shine a candle to Dennis. I would make love to my girlfriend, in between her increasingly strident exhortations for me to marry her, and, seconds after my release, would berate myself for having the gall to enjoy pleasures of the flesh while my brother's body was cold, dead, in the ground, and decaying at a rapid rate. I would talk to my family, my parents and siblings both, like a robot in a science fiction movie; I had nothing to say and no ability to listen. They too, for the moment, seemed dead to me.

Worse were the conversations with prospective clients. I would stare at them intently when they would begin to tell their stories, doing my best to feign both interest and compassion. They would outline their problems, but before getting too far along, I would tune them out. Nodding and shaking my head at the wrong times; responding to their impassioned pleas with stone cold silence; staring vacantly into space while they bared their souls; I was an extraordinarily insensitive and ineffective lawyer.

Needless to say, I was bringing in little money for the firm of Tucci & Semes. I recruited none of my own clients, not a one. The only work I was doing had been derived from the firm's existing client base and that work was infrequent and non-sustaining. Allen and Michael, aware of my personal tragedy, were kind but their compassion had limits. Pursuant to our agreement, I was paid in proportion to my contributions to the firm. After a few months, my income stream had hit a roadblock. I still did not care enough to try and make any changes.

I had rented a lovely first floor one bedroom apartment in the town of Ardmore, on the Main Line, close to Route 30 (the main thoroughfare) and the suburban train station which took me to and from work every day. The apartment came with a living room fireplace, rich mahogany wood paneling, a full-size bed, a large clothing dresser, a table, a lamp, and an old wooden chair. I did not buy or borrow a single piece of furniture, as I was content with the sparse furnishings provided by my landlord.

As the summer wore on and my income dwindled, I was left with insufficient funds to pay for my basic needs. I told no one about my financial plight and did not ask anyone for a loan to help get me on my feet. I derived my nutrients from a steady diet of macaroni and cheese and Doritos. My phone service was shut off first, which I did not mind much, as it gave me a good excuse to curtail my burdensome communications. But it was not such an easy transition when the gas and electric were turned off for non-payment.

I found out that it is not easy to read in the dark. I tried candle-light, Abe Lincoln style, but the unsteady flicker would give me a headache after I read for about thirty minutes. So once or twice a week I would walk to Villanova Law School, my alma mater, about a mile and a half from my apartment, for comfortable reading in good light. I would go straight to the basement of the well-lit library, with its comfortable couches, read a book until one or two in the morning and then start my thirty minute trek back to my dark apartment.

One late evening in May 1994, a young Villanova undergraduate walked beside me for about half a mile. For some reason, I decided to engage in small talk.

"So how do you like Villanova so far?"

"Great. It's a lot of fun. I'm having a blast."

"Where are you from?"

"Brooklyn. New York."

"Me, too. Small world. What high school did you go to?"

"Poly Prep."

"You've got to be kidding me. That's my alma mater."

"Cool. What year did you graduate?"

"1982."

"Do you know Larry Patton? He was one of my favorite teachers."

"Of course I know Larry. We played together on the offensive line. He was a guard, I was a tackle. Larry was a damn good football player ... but I thought he was in banking."

"He was. But he quit banking to become a teacher. He used to joke that banking was rotting his soul. He's an amazing teacher. He really connected with the students. Hey, this is my street ... see you later."

As the young man peeled off Route 30, I harkened back to my days at Poly Prep, where Dennis and I had formed our own clique of two. Funny how fate works. Larry Patton was back teaching at Poly Prep;

Dennis was in the ground; and I was a modern, wannabe Henry David Thoreau, a minimalist with the need for just a touch of modern comforts (like electricity). No one would have believed that a mere four years earlier I had been the Commencement Speaker for my graduating law school class. Small world, indeed.

In July, I took the Pennsylvania bar exam. When I had taken the New York bar exam four years earlier, my roommate, John Lutz, and I had driven to Albany the day before. We ate dinner at a swanky Italian restaurant and stayed in a comfortable hotel. John slept like a log but I was so nervous and anxious that I did not sleep at all. Instead I watched a West Coast baseball game on ESPN. Ramon Martinez pitched for the Dodgers. I can't remember anything else about that game, except that I was surprised that the soothing voice of Vin Scully did not help me get to sleep.

The Pennsylvania bar exam was a different experience altogether. I had purchased two train tokens for the ride to Philadelphia and then back to Ardmore. That left me with about twenty-five cents to my name. Just enough for a phone call in the event of my arrest. Even though I had barely studied for the Pennsylvania exam, I was not the least bit nervous. I arrived at the Philadelphia Convention Center well-rested and strangely confident.

The bar exam is comprised of two equally weighted parts: the multi-state section (given to law students throughout the nation) consists of one hundred difficult multiple choice questions on basic areas of law; the essay section requires analyses of a multitude of wide-ranging legal issues. Each section lasts four hours and the test-takers are allotted a one hour lunch break after the multi-state.

After I completed the multi-state, I milled about outside the convention center amidst a jungle of mid-exam law students, each with a carefully wrapped lunch. I realized that I had not brought any lunch, had not eaten breakfast or dinner the night before, and was famished to the point of distraction. I sat down against the wall for a few minutes but when I tried to stand up I almost fell over. I was dizzy and light-headed; this was no way to take a test.

Like a scavenger, I circled the building for discarded scraps of food. I was lucky enough to find a banana and half of a peanut butter and jelly sandwich, which I wolfed down without regard to taste or texture. Food as fuel. After the test, when the law students disbursed, some of them hugged and comforted each other. I didn't say a word to anyone before hopping on the train that would take me back to my Main Line dungeon.

In August the heat grew stifling. I would sit in my bed, naked, as sweat dripped down my head, chest, and—when it was really hot—my legs. My electric fan, reduced to an impotent prop, stood but a few feet from the edge of my bed just to tease me. When I could stand it no more I took a shower. I made sure to pay my water bill. After all, I was not an animal.

For entertainment, I would go to the movies. The Ardmore Theater (on Route 30) was an old-fashioned, one-screen theater, already a dinosaur in the age of the multiplex. In 1994 the movie *Forrest Gump* played all summer. I know this because I saw the film about thirty times. When my money ran out, I would enter the theater, head straight for the bathroom, linger for a few minutes, and then walk into the screening room. After a while, when I began to be recognized by the kid ticket puncher, I would just nod to him and walk into the theater as if I owned the joint.

Forrest Gump featured a scene where Lieutenant Dan (played by Gary Sinise), who lost his legs in Vietnam, shouted his outrage at God—from the mast of a shrimping boat—in the midst of a violent storm. I envied his ability to express his rage. In the face of my silence, my soul was fomenting like a once great bottle of wine that had soured right in front of me. It was turning into vinegar, if not urine, before my eyes and I was powerless to do anything to stop it from infecting me to the core. I was not just angry at God. I was mad at the world and everyone in it; I was mad at myself for not being strong enough to save the person in the world whom I loved the most; and most of all I was enraged at Dennis for leaving me alone in the chaos to fend for myself. The sweetness of life had a sour, bitter taste which I could not expunge.

Some time in August, made emptier by the absence of baseball, Mike Semes called me into his office to chat. Mike was an ethical, decent man with a strong Christian faith and a wife and several daughters whom he adored. He was blossoming as an attorney, as his clients respected his diligence, honesty, and no-nonsense approach.

"Congratulations, Kevin," he said, "we just found out you passed the Pennsylvania bar." The news barely registered with me and my non-reaction surprised and confused him.

"Thanks, Mike," I said. "I appreciate everything you've done for me."

Mike stood up from his chair behind the desk, closed the door, and sat down in a plush leather guest chair right next to me. "We need you to pick up the pace, my friend . . . we know you can do it . . . we know how hard a year you've had since what happened to your brother."

"Do you really know what happened?" I replied.

Mike straightened in his chair and lowered his voice to barely above a whisper. He placed a hand gently on my shoulder. "I know he was sick . . . AND I KNOW HE DROWNED HIMSELF."

I recoiled at the words and Mike quickly pulled back his hand. I KNOW HE DROWNED HIMSELF. I couldn't get that phrase out of my head. Mike had provided me with a window into the conventional wisdom as to the end of Dennis. The genie was out of the bottle. Dennis Mulhearn went crazy and killed himself. That was the one sentence epitaph written for my brother by my friends and peers. Everyone did the arithmetic and concluded suicide by drowning. Mike was the first person with the candor to clue me in to the calculation.

I figured all of this from five simple words whispered by my friend and boss: I KNOW HE DROWNED HIMSELF.

To most people the nuances of Dennis's death meant nothing. As the theorem called Occam's Razor instructs scientists, when faced with a number of possible explanations for an occurrence, the simplest explanation is usually the best. Here, the poor boy went nuts and checked out early. Occam's Razor at its simplest and most straighforward. To me, though, the simplicity of this assessment was false in the extremis. The placement of the suicide tag on my brother offended his honor, decency, and courage. Dennis was an affirmation of life. He was both far too tough, and too gentle, to just kill himself.

But I did not know that for sure. An ugly, awful doubt lingered: Did the ravages of mental illness overwhelm Dennis's will to the point where he believed that he had no choice but to end his life? Or, more extravagantly, did Dennis believe that he was a modern version of Christ who needed to die in order to be resurrected . . . to prove his divinity to the world, or, maybe, to himself?

These questions kept me from sleeping on many a night, but, as hard as I tried, I could never find a definitive, satisfactory answer to them.

The word "suicide," with all of its ramifications for my Roman Catholic family, was not one any of us would dare raise. Ever. But for me, for more than a decade, the word hung in the air like a rancid fish, always ready to ruin my day, always lurking underneath the veil of potential joy. The threshold question tugged at me—day and night—without mercy: what the hell was Dennis doing when he jumped into the water with full knowledge that he swam like a rock?

When I resigned from Tucci & Semes several weeks later, Allen and Mike were kind enough to forgive several hundred dollars of personal debts that I had racked up on the firm's accounts. I never even had to explain to them why I needed to leave, for they both knew as well as I that in 1994 I had no business practicing law in Philadelphia.

More than a year had passed since Dennis had drowned, and I needed, finally, desperately, to go home. To my family. To my father.

CHAPTER TWENTY-SIX

No Words

Give sorrow words; the grief that does not speak knits up the o-er wrought heart and bids it break.

— William Shakespeare, *Macbeth*

My time in Ardmore and Philadelphia—in 1994—is now mostly a blur. I am blessed with an exceptional memory but can remember few details about the first half of that year. I do know, however, that as I grieved the death of my brother, I sank deeper and deeper into an unhealthy state of isolation. My Philadelphia sojourn was pulling me away from my family and all things I cherished.

But like a hiker stuck in a patch of quicksand, I could not figure out on my own how to extricate myself from my rapidly deteriorating condition. I lacked the resolve and clear-mindedness necessary to make a rational, positive decision to improve my lot, to begin to reconnect, to start, at least, on the path to happiness.

Then, in or about August 1994, serendipity struck. I was disqualified as an attorney in a case that was set for trial. And that disqualification, that procedural defeat, was the impetus that changed the entire trajectory of my life.

Earlier that year I had agreed to file a lawsuit on behalf of my dad's wife, Willie, against her ex-husband and the lawyer who, by himself, had handled their divorce. Her ex-husband, a union construction worker, had a valuable and vested pension with his employer. Willie was legally entitled to about half of that pension, a pretty decent sum. But the divorce agreement made no mention of the pension. She claimed that the lawyer never told her that she was entitled to receive any portion of the pension. Her ex-husband and the lawyer claimed that they had discussed this issue with Willie and she had agreed to waive her pension interest. The divorce agreement itself was silent on the issue and never even referenced the pension. So, on these facts, I filed a lawsuit in the Rockland County Supreme Court to modify the divorce agreement and to include the pension, or a monetary equivalent, as part of the equitable distribution package between Willie and her ex-husband.

As I was still living in Ardmore and working for Tucci & Semes in Philadelphia, I used my father and Willie's apartment as my New York office address and their home phone number as my office phone. But, just weeks before the trial was scheduled to begin, David Bushman, Willie's ex-husband's lawyer, made a motion to the Court, pursuant to an obscure New York law, which sought to disqualify me as Willie's attorney for failure to maintain a bona fide law office in New York State. As I had no defense, and Bushman was right on the law, the Court granted the motion and just like that I was off the case.

My father then came up with a simple yet elegant solution to the problem. I would open a New York office, as cheaply as possible, and stay in Nanuet with him and Willie in their one bedroom apartment for a few weeks, just until the trial was over.

My dad contacted the Rockland County Bar Association and discovered that a Rockland attorney, Sanford "Sandy" Cohen, was looking to rent a small office in Orangeburg, New York, at the southern tip of Rockland County. My father met with Sandy, a grizzled, veteran lawyer and chain-smoker, and haggled over the price of the monthly rent. Sandy agreed to the price of $400.00 a month and my father, even before consulting with me about this strategy, shook hands with Sandy and closed the deal for a no lease, month-to-month rental agreement.

When my father presented this option to me I wasn't keen about sharing a one bedroom apartment—with but one bathroom—with my dad and his wife, but, floundering in Philadelphia, still without electricity, I agreed to this arrangement. My quick assent to my father's plan reflected my inability to take control over my own life. I was no longer controlling circumstances. Circumstances were controlling me. So I rolled with the tide and agreed to live with my father . . . for just a few weeks.

I left Philadelphia, said goodbye and thank you to Allen and Mike, and began my anticipated short career as a New York sole practitioner. My office, located on the second floor of Prel Plaza, a small strip mall building with a lovely view of Clausland Mountain, proved the old adage that you get what you pay for. For my $400.00 a month, I received an office the size of a broom closet. Swallowed by the desk in the middle of the room, the office could seat me and one guest comfortably; two, if they both weighed less than two hundred pounds.

But, as I gained my bearings in New York, I soon realized that I liked Sandy Cohen quite a bit. He was pleasant, sharp, kind, and had a wonderful dry sense of humor. He was always willing to share his hard-earned knowledge of the law—not just as written in the books, but how it really worked—with me. From the start, Sandy made me feel at home. He also gave me a shot of confidence when I desperately needed it.

I didn't even mind, too much, at least, the thin layer of smoke that perpetually wafted through the air and into my nostrils and onto my clothes. Sandy, for some reason, began to call me "Doctor," and, for some reason, I kind of liked the sound of that word. Ensconced in Orangeburg, I began, for the first time in a long while, to concentrate with laser focus on the legal matters I was handling.

Soon after I settled into Prel Plaza, I made a motion to the Rockland County Supreme Court to be reinstated as Willie's attorney in her pending case. In or about September 1994, the Court granted my motion and we were back in business. But the trial kept getting pushed back, so my stay at Nanuet, too, kept getting extended. The most burdensome part of this arrangement was my lack of a car. Rockland County, with its limited and slow bus system, demanded a vehicle in which to get around. But I didn't own one; so I was forced to rely on my father to drop me off at and pick me up from my office.

My dad often came to pick me up before I was finished with my work. But, stripped of autonomy over my schedule, I didn't have any choice. I needed to leave when I needed to leave and that was that. Although I was thirty-years-old, this arrangement made me feel like a teenager. In many ways I had regressed. I was dependent on my father for most of my basic needs: food, shelter, and transportation.

But there was also a flip side to this coin. My father and I started to talk to each other again. Even though our conversations usually centered around the nuances of baseball or some other sport, rather than the emotional upheaval that we had undergone the last few years, we began to connect again as father and son. He was no longer a stranger to me. He was my father again.

As an adult living with my father, I was far more perceptive and critical than I had been as a child. My father had many flaws which were crystallized by our daily interaction: he was extraordinarily judgmental, close-minded—once he decided something it stayed decided, no matter how much evidence was presented to contradict his view or position—, a slave to his routines, and quick to attack any person who challenged or even questioned his opinions, judgments, or decisions, on matters grave or trivial.

But my recognition of my father's faults did not diminish the love and respect I had for him. Quite to the contrary, after I moved in with my dad, I soon realized that he was my biggest advocate, my most vocal champion, and my protector. My father never told me to my face what he thought of me. He just wasn't built like that. That was just not his way. But I found out from about a half dozen of his friends who came to me, at my dad's behest, for legal services, that he had practically begged them to call me, that he told them I was bright but, most importantly, fundamentally honest and decent, and could be trusted to do the right thing. For Dad, who was stingy with compliments, that was high praise.

My father never complained about the length of my stay in Nanuet. Or about how I was draining his savings. Or about my destruction of his privacy with his wife. I think that he kind of liked having me around. I was his most immediate link to the past, filled with much love and high achievements, along with the devastating disappointments and indescribable tragedy.

The worst moment in his life was the death of my brother. My daily presence in my father's life did not do much to ease his pain over the loss of his son—nothing could; but he was at least able to keep an eye out for me, to guide me through my struggles, and to do everything in his power to keep me from harm's reach.

When I was a child, my father always made me feel safe. When I was with him, I always felt invincible. I believed that my father, who almost always carried his service revolver in an ankle holster, would do whatever it took to protect me from evil in all of its forms. I soon felt kind of the same way, even though I now realized that my father was not infallible, after I moved in with him in the Fall of 1994. That sense of security had been missing during my self-imposed period of isolation in Pennsylvania.

My dad also pushed me, incessantly and without apology, to challenge myself, to not accept mediocrity, and to reach for my full potential. Second-rate, half-assed, effort, in anything I did, was not acceptable—no matter how great my loss or how sharp my pain. There were no excuses. If a job needed to be done, I needed to try my best to do it right. My father reminded me, over and over, that my effort was the only thing that

I could *always* control. Others often dictated the outcome, the end result, but I, and only I, determined how hard I was going to fight for anything, any person, any cause, that I believed merited my support or advocacy.

My father, in 1994 and 1995, taught me—without ever saying so directly—that although Dennis was gone, I needed to move forward, to live my life, and to strive for happiness and success. My father never stopped believing in me. Not once. And because he never quit on me, I never seriously contemplated quitting on myself.

My father also helped me fill, at least at the edges, the gigantic, gaping hole in my heart. And I don't know if anyone else could have done that quite the way he did: with sharp humor, high intelligence, unwavering faith in my ability, and repeated assurances that I would eventually find my way. Dad was my landing rock, my salvation, and—after Dennis died—my best friend. It was most comforting to realize that there was at least one man in the universe who would do anything within his power for me to grow up and be a happy, fulfilled, content, man. Not a boy, but a man.

Professionally, I struggled mightily that first year. I didn't know anyone from Rockland County and I was thus able to pick up business only in scraps, in bits and pieces—a will here, a lease there. Sandy had a lifetime of good legal forms for me to plagiarize—which is perfectly acceptable in the law—and, as was often the case, when I didn't have a clue as to how to proceed, he usually pointed me in the right direction.

My gross income for my first year as a sole practitioner was less than $12,000.00. I lived frugally and simply, working in Orangeburg during the day and watching sports and talking with my dad in Nanuet at night.

Willie treated me like a prince. She was always kind and generous to me, never had a cross word, and came to accept my ubiquitous presence in her cramped apartment.

By October 8, 1995, my several weeks stay at my father and Willie's Nanuet apartment had extended to a little more than a year. (I would stay there for another six months). I had recently purchased my first car, a blue Nissan Sentra, which gave me a lot more independence. But on this cool autumn evening, my dad and I were glued to the living room television, rooting for the Yankees to take the deciding Game Five of a riveting, back and forth playoff series between the Yankees and the Seattle Mariners.

Buck Showalter, the Yankees' manager, had seemed to blow a gasket in this series, which marked the first time the Yanks had been in the playoffs since losing the 1982 World Series to the Los Angeles Dodgers in six games. After winning the first two games at home, the Yankees had lost two in a row at the raucous Seattle Kingdome. This was the first and only playoff appearance for Yankees' legend and Mulhearn boys' favorite, Don Mattingly, and he played and hit well throughout the series. But not quite well enough.

John Wetteland, the Yankees' closer, had struggled throughout the series, giving up several runs in the first two games and four runs without getting a single out in the Game Four loss the night before. Showalter lost confidence in Wetteland and decided keep him in the bullpen for the duration of Game Five.

Resembling Captain Queeg in a baseball cap, rotating metal ball bearings in his hand again and again as the game leaked into extra innings, Showalter trusted only three pitchers with the season on the line: David Cone, a stud righthander in his prime, Mariano Rivera, a twenty-five year old rookie with guts and moxie to go along with a great rising fastball—this was several years before Mariano discovered, by serendipity, his cut fastball (a.k.a. the "cutter"), a devastating pitch that at the last moment broke sharply in to lefties and away from righties—, and, finally, Jack McDowell, a lanky, anti-social, give-the-bird-to-the-fans, righthander just past his prime.

In the top of the eleventh inning, the Yankees pushed across the go ahead run against future Hall of Famer Randy Johnson on a walk, a sacrifice bunt, and a single by the Yankees' second baseman, Randy Velarde, between short and third. Now leading 5 to 4, the Yankees needed just three more outs to move on to the American League Championship Series against the Cleveland Indians.

Joey Cora, the Mariners' second baseman, led off the bottom of the inning against Black Jack McDowell (not Wetteland) with a just good enough drag bunt to Don Mattingly at first, and twisted at the last second to barely elude Mattingly's attempted tag. Ken Griffey Jr. then lined a hard single to right just past the desperate lunge of Velarde to make it first and third with no outs. The next batter, Yankees' killer Edgar Martinez, lined a fastball down the left field line. Cora scored easily and Ken Griffey raced around the bases like a man possessed. Griffey slid safely into home as the throw from the outfield bounced harmlessly in front of the Yankees' catcher, Jim Leyritz.

The Seattle players mobbed both Griffey and Martinez and, after saluting the Kingdome fans for their vocal support, marched jubilantly off the field with a 6-5 win. In Nanuet my father and I sat back. We were both stunned and disappointed and didn't say anything to each other for a few minutes.

When at last my father turned to me to speak, his steel blue eyes moist, glazed, and red around the rims, he asked, "what the hell was your brother thinking when he jumped into the water?"

I looked at him again. He was beseeching me to give him an answer that would comfort him and alleviate his pain. But I could not muster any reassuring answer.

"I don't know, Dad . . . I just don't know," I mumbled. He looked at me, nodded, and then turned away and changed the television channel.

That one minute conversation with my father was the first and only time we ever talked about Dennis's death while I lived under my dad's roof. It was just too damn painful. There were no answers. No words. No comfort. That was his burden. And mine.

Part Three:

Jackals' Justice

Did it matter whom it might crush to death on its mad course?
Was it not, after all, heading for the future, careless of the blood
it might spill along the way? Driver-less, like a maddened beast,
it rushed on and on with its load of cannon-fodder.

And the soldiers, drunk and dazed with fatigue, were singing as
they went.

— Emile Zola, *The Beast in Man*

Jackal

1. Any of several nocturnal wild dogs of the genus *Canis,* es-
    pecially *C. aureus,* of Asia and Africa, that scavenge or hunt
    in packs.

2. A person who performs dishonest or base deeds as the fol-
    lower or accomplice of another.

3. A person who performs menial or degrading tasks for an-
    other.[12]

CHAPTER TWENTY-SEVEN

Law and Truth

If ... the machine of government ... is of such a nature that it requires you to be the agent of injustice to another, then, I say, break the law. Let your life be a counter friction to stop the machine.

— Henry David Thoreau, *Civil Disobedience*

Truth. The word is ubiquitous in law. A trial is supposed to be a search for the truth. Every witness swears to tell the truth, the whole truth, and nothing but the truth. So help me God. But in the law business, God must be a busy man—because the truth is often buried or blurred by bare knuckle tactics, political considerations, or noxious legal principles which have gained the force of law.

The petty falsehoods, the white lies told by every lawyer, including me (either personally or through surrogates)—he's not in right now, I won't take a penny less than $50,000.00, the law is crystal clear on this point—threaten to swallow the more honorable aspects of the profession. Worse yet, the small lies can so easily lead to far greater deceits. When one gets comfortable telling lies there is a natural progression of falsity which has a unique and compelling power. I am constantly on guard against this syndrome but sometimes my vigilance is not as strong as it needs to be. Like all of us, I remain a work in progress.

Still, at its most pure, the law can be an invigorating splash of hope and humanity. A lawyer who fights for elusive justice for his wronged client, particularly when the odds are stacked against him, makes a real difference. At least that's what I've been telling myself for more than two decades. Hindsight being sharp, I often question the wisdom of some of my more quixotic choices. In the end, was the battle worth it?

I asked myself early in my legal career another penetrating question: can a good man, an honest man, be a good lawyer? The answer is not as obvious as it may seem at first blush as no one can fall easily or neatly into all, or any, of those categories. The law, like the world, is filled with shades of gray, rather than its starker cousins, black and white.

For explication, I imagine posing this hypothetical to recent law school graduates who come looking for a job: A man walks into your office minutes after he has kidnapped a twelve-year-old girl and buried her alive in a wooden box in a field about a mile away. He sits down and asks for assurances that everything he tells you will be kept confidential. You assure him that the attorney-client privilege protects him as you may not and will not disclose any information about any crimes that he has committed to anyone else. He then tells you his story, specifies where the girl is buried, and tells you that she has about three more hours to live before she will suffocate. He pays you a retainer, leaves your office, and tells you he is driving up to Canada to start a new life. You have researched this subject in depth and know that the law in your state precludes you from revealing any information about the girl's location to the police or anyone else, and that if you breach the attorney-client privilege and contact law enforcement authorities, you will be disbarred. What would you do?

Many of these applicants would probably tell me what they thought I wanted to hear. The law is sacrosanct, as is the protection of the basic rights of a client, the most basic of which is the protection of confidential, potentially incriminating information. So the good lawyer must keep his mouth shut, let the girl die, and suffer the consequences of a wounded conscience as the steep but necessary price to uphold the integrity of his profession. If I had any say in the matter, though, these young lawyers would be still pounding the pavement.

The answer I would want to hear is this: I could not live with the thought that I could have saved an innocent little girl but consciously chose to let her die in order to uphold a legal principle. I would call the police ten seconds after the perpetrator left my office and then head straight to the field with a shovel to help with the digging. If the powers-that-be would ultimately determine that I had committed a disbarrable offense, then so be it. I would roll up my sleeves and start working in another profession.

The latter group would refuse to surrender their humanity to the law. They are people first, lawyers second. These are my type of lawyers. They are willing to follow their own personal code of right and wrong and ignore, when necessary, laws that instruct them otherwise. That is the only way the law can be practiced with morality.

Although the point seems both incongruent and heretical, my experience teaches me that it is the gospel truth: the moral practice of law requires a lawyer to place his own value system above the black and white letter of the law, above the myriad rules of law, and above legal precedent. The law is not static but fluid; it is, ultimately, whatever one can shape with his best efforts to serve the greater good. The law, at its best, when a lawyer's value system is strong and worthy, is a vehicle for justice and yes . . . I'll use the word again, truth.

But the search for truth is never easy. In my hypothetical, the moral lawyer has to lie to do the right thing. He has given the kidnapper and soon-to-be murderer his solemn word that he will not break his confidences and his sworn duty is to uphold the law. So he must lie to arrive at a more precious and fundamental truth: an innocent child deserves to escape from a gruesome death. Even truth then arrives in shades and degrees. It is often cloaked for those who seek it, and those who do not consciously seek truth will rarely, if ever, catch even a glimpse of it.

Of course, too often the law is nothing but a slave to the status quo. Then, the law may be an agent for injustice, a conduit of pain, or an instrument of evil. The law is, far too frequently, the enemy of truth.

The battle lines of the law are never drawn as clearly as they may seem. But the consequences of a lawyer's choices, his decisions on whether he will serve the law or make the law serve him, are often profound.

I, for one, was never content to be a servant.

CHAPTER TWENTY-EIGHT

A Snowball's Chance

in Hell

Once you make a decision, the universe conspires to make it happen.

— Ralph Waldo Emerson

On Sunday morning, November 20, 2005, I bought the *New York Post* at the gas station convenience store across the street from Prel Plaza and headed to my office to work on a case. I expected to work for a few hours and get home in time to watch the afternoon football games. When I arrived at my office and flipped the *Post* to its front cover, I was surprised to see the snarling image of Phil Foglietta, Poly Prep's late, iconic football coach, as he was walking off Poly's football field.

The headline blared, "Prestigious Poly Prep Grid Great's Abuse Drove Me to Drugs and Despair." The author of the story—a photo of whom was inside the paper—was David Hiltbrand, a clean-cut, handsome man, who identified himself as a 1971 graduate of Poly Prep.

David told a harrowing tale of abuse, beginning with his initial pride that Foglietta—a renowned youth sports leader in Bay Ridge and Sunset

Park—was paying special attention to him, developing into his appreciation of the access Foglietta gave him and other kids to the sparkling Poly
Prep athletic facilities, and culminating in Foglietta's assault of Hiltbrand
and other boys in the "steam room" showers in Poly's locker room.[13]

He then described how his abuse by Foglietta filled him with "self-
loathing," turned him away from sports, and propelled him to begin using hard drugs in an effort to numb his pain. David Hiltbrand recounted
that he was "a hopeless addict" by the time he turned thirteen.[14]

David wrote that he had talked to many Foglietta victims, and that,
in time, Foglietta's sexual assaults had escalated to sodomy and rape.[15]
That statement, which made me realize that some of my Poly school-
mates had been dragged into a living hell, shocked, disgusted, and enraged me.

In early 1991, David Hiltbrand wrote a poignant and heart-breaking
letter to Poly Prep's then headmaster, William M. Williams, and informed him that he had been sexually abused by Phil Foglietta, while a
student at Poly Prep. For weeks, David waited, to no avail, for a response. Then, some weeks later, when David was visiting his parents in
Brooklyn, he called Headmaster Williams and Williams—no doubt to
his considerable regret—picked up the phone. Williams told David Hiltbrand that he had been unable to respond to his letter because he had
hurt his hand skiing, and—to David's horror and outrage—that Phil Foglietta was still on Poly Prep's faculty.[16]

In September 1991, after Foglietta's "retirement" from Poly Prep,
which was apparently compelled by a complaint from a *current* Poly Prep
student in 1991, the school threw Foglietta a lavish retirement party at
the Downtown Athletic Club in New York City. I remembered receiving a fancy, engraved invitation to that party. I had given serious consid-
eration to attending but at the last minute, besieged with work, I decided
to stay home.

David's contempt for this farewell gala was stark and completely un-
derstandable: "I'm told speaker after speaker—to the applause of some

500 guests—praised the guy who raped innocent little boys on school grounds." [17]

At the end of his article, David Hiltbrand referenced a lawsuit recently filed by John Joseph "J." Paggioli against Poly Prep. That was the first time I had heard of J. Paggioli or his lawsuit.

David's article both intrigued and angered me. He accused Poly Prep of keeping Foglietta on staff with full knowledge of his crimes against children.[18] There but for the grace of God go I, or my brothers, I thought.

How could this have happened? How could so many good people and highly respected educators have allowed Phil Foglietta to assault and rape innocent little boys for twenty-five years?

There were no acceptable answers to these questions. My plans for the day had changed. I would not be watching any football. In a flurry of activity, I began researching the facts and the law on Poly Prep's potential legal culpability for facilitating the sexual abuse of its students.

For starters, I read a number of recent articles in various New York papers and other media outlets: the *New York Daily News*, the *New York Post*, the *New York Times*, *Newsday*, *WINS 1010 AM News Radio*, and *Fox News TV*, which discussed the lawsuit filed by J. Paggioli. Apparently, in April, 2004, J. Paggioli had filed a lawsuit in Kings County Supreme Court against Poly Prep and several of its former and current administrators for concealing information about Foglietta and his sexual abuse of students. He went public about his suit for the first time on September 30, 2005 in "the hope of helping any other victims." [19]

After some articles were published about the case in the *Daily News* in early October 2005, John Marino, a Poly Prep football player in the early 1970s, came forward to J. Paggioli and his counsel—Marc Fliedner—and stated that he personally observed Coach Foglietta—on numerous occasions—engage in oral sex with young boys in Foglietta's green Impala, a block away from Poly Prep.[20] (I knew John Marino's younger brother, Joseph, a Class of 1984 graduate of Poly Prep. My brothers and I took the bus with Joe to and from Poly Prep for two years. Joe was a feisty kid who made no attempt to hide his contempt for Coach Foglietta and several other Poly Prep coaches).

John Marino, a psychiatrist in upstate New York, provided Paggioli with a statement that attested to those observations and also claimed that he and his parents told Poly Prep administrators, Headmaster William Williams and Athletic Director Harlow Parker, about Foglietta's sexual abuse of children but that Williams and Parker dismissed his allegations out-of-hand and did nothing.[21]

My blood boiled over these charges because John Marino claimed that he reported Foglietta's sexual misconduct in the early 1970s and Foglietta continued to work at Poly Prep until 1991. How many kids were assaulted by Phil Foglietta over those two decades after Poly Prep administrators knew or at least should have known that he was a sexual predator?

The newspaper articles indicated that Poly Prep had made a motion to dismiss J. Paggioli's Complaint on statute of limitations grounds. A November 17, 2005 article in the *New York Times*,[22] claimed that a hearing on the defendants' motion to dismiss had taken place just the day before (November 16, 2005).

Jeffrey Kohn, a partner at O'Melveny & Myers, LLP, and Poly Prep's lawyer, was quoted by the *Times* as saying that the statute of limitations was an impenetrable bar: "If you look at some recent cases in the past year against a number of other institutions, including churches, non-profits, schools, the New York law very, very clearly states that any kind of claim of repressed memory for so many years" does not override the statute of limitations.[23]

So, according to Jeffrey Kohn, it was "very, very clear" that J. Paggioli had no case because he had waited too long to file suit.

The *Times* ended its article as follows: "Mr. Kohn said yesterday that he was focused only on the statute of limitations issue and not on the merits of the suit, although he added that the school would deny the allegations if the case went ahead."[24]

That last lawyer statement ticked me off: "the school would deny the allegations" if the case survived the motion to dismiss. Poly Prep was stating through its counsel that it would simply deny the allegations of John Marino, a reputable psychiatrist, and anyone else who came forward and claimed that Poly Prep officials knew about, and thus facilitated, Phil Foglietta's sexual abuse of children. The best defense was a good offense. Poly Prep intended to play hardball.

Where was my school's compassion for J. Paggioli and the other victims of Phil Foglietta? I couldn't see it.

Screw you, we'll just deny everything. That was the school's public response to childhood sex abuse survivors. Jesus, I thought, Poly Prep— the school that preached constantly that character was king—was, or certainly should have been, better than that.

After I read every online article about Poly Prep, J. Paggioli, and Phil Foglietta, I turned to my trusty legal research tool: Westlaw. I started with the statute of limitations issue and quickly realized that on this point, at least, Jeffrey Kohn was right: J. Paggioli had little or no chance to circumvent the applicable statutes of limitations for his asserted claims against Poly Prep and its officials.

Now what? Back to square one. For my search parameters I typed in "sex abuse" and "Civil RICO" and was guided to a fascinating case that had recently been filed, and summarily dismissed (in 2005), in the U.S. District Court for the Northern District of New York.

In *Hatfield v. Tyson*,[**] the plaintiff, Scott Hatfield, brought suit against an upstate priest, Father Dilbert Tyson, and various officials of and at-

---

[**] To protect the innocent and the not-so-innocent alike, all names in this case, including those in the case title, have been changed to pseudonyms.

torneys for a local diocese, on the grounds that the defendants had con-
spired and acted to cover-up Father Tyson's sexual abuse of Hatfield.

The facts of this case, taken from Hatfield's complaint and Civil
RICO statement (as summarized by the federal court in its opinion),
were bizarre and disturbing. At the time Hatfield met Father Tyson, he
was homeless, destitute, and involved in drugs and prostitution. Father
Tyson befriended him and eventually provided room and board, as well
as a maintenance job for him in Father Tyson's rectory, for about four
years (from 1998-2002). During that time, Hatfield enrolled in college
and began studying to be a teacher.

Father Tyson portrayed his relationship with Hatfield as one between father and son. But Hatfield claimed that Father Tyson sexually
abused and molested him at various times for the four years he lived and
worked at the rectory. Hatfield claimed that while he did not condone
or consent to the sexual conduct, he offered no resistance because he
was afraid of losing the financial security that Father Tyson provided.

In August of 1992, Hatfield accused Father Tyson of sexual abuse and
attempted to negotiate a civil settlement which would provide him with
some money for the abuse he had endured.

He met with Father Tyson and various Church officials to discuss his
claims. At one meeting, the Bishop in charge instructed Father Tyson to
continue to pay Hatfield's food and rent stipend at his university until
the civil matter was resolved or settled. Father Tyson complied with this
edict.

Weeks later, there was another meeting between Hatfield and
Church officials where Hatfield accepted a $75,000.00 settlement offer
from Father Tyson as payment in full for any and all claims. This
agreement, however, was not put in writing by an attorney for the
Church until more than four months after the offer was made and accepted.

Then the worm turned. Several months after the parties agreed on
settlement terms, Father Tyson, now represented by a different attor-

ney, filed criminal charges against Hatfield for attempted felony extortion. Father Tyson claimed that Hatfield repeatedly threatened to go to the media with his story if he did not receive some money. Father Tyson and the Church officials continued to "negotiate" an alleged civil settlement with Hatfield, who was unaware that felony charges had been filed against him.

A local police officer, Detective Smith, began working with Church employees during his investigation of the extortion charges against Hatfield, and went so far as to secretly tape record Hatfield's conversations with the Church's secretary. During this time period, Hatfield claimed that Church officials repeatedly told him that his settlement money was coming soon.

In August 2003, Detective Smith took Hatfield into custody and interrogated him for an hour—without a lawyer—about the alleged extortion. The interrogation was taped. The next day Hatfield attended a "mediation" meeting and was told that Father Tyson no longer intended to pay him $75,000.00, or, for that matter, one red cent. Hatfield then attempted to file criminal charges against Father Tyson but Detective Smith—the same officer investigating the "extortion" charge against Hatfield—forbade him from doing so.

In October 2003, Hatfield was arrested and indicted by an upstate New York grand jury for Attempted Grand Larceny in the Second Degree, a felony. A month later, Hatfield was forced to withdraw from school. And, because he had been indicted on a felony, he was also forced to withdraw from his student teaching position.

Three months later, in February 2004, the Court dismissed the indictment against Hatfield in "the interest of justice." The judge explained that the case against Hatfield was full of holes: Hatfield never received any money; the settlement negotiations that occurred tended to negate the requisite criminal intent; Father Tyson was reluctant to testify; punishment would unlikely effect Hatfield's character; and the "crime" was unlikely to be repeated.

The judge nevertheless made it a point to note the propriety of the indictment. He emphasized that the record before the grand jury was unusually full and complete, and that Hatfield's testimony had been both "ambiguous" and "harmful to his interests."

On these facts, Hatfield filed his civil action in federal court in August 2004 (just a few months after J. Paggioli file his initial Complaint against Poly Prep in Kings County Supreme Court). Hatfield alleged that the defendants had violated Civil RICO by conducting or participating in the conduct of an enterprise's affairs through a pattern of racketeering activity (and conspiring to do so).[25]

Hatfield alleged that the "racketeering activities" which triggered Civil RICO liability included "mail fraud," which is defined simply and broadly as the use of the mail to further "any scheme or artifice to defraud, or for obtaining money or property by means of false and fraudulent pretenses."[26]

The federal court in *Hatfield v. Tyson* destroyed Hatfield's Civil RICO causes of action. The judge picked apart the Complaint, RICO element by RICO element, like a hawk picking at the carcass of a woodchuck, until nothing was left of Hatfield's Civil RICO claims.

But, on the afternoon of November 20, 2005, I was encouraged, rather than discouraged. Although Scott Hatfield had not pled Civil RICO to the extent necessary to survive a motion to dismiss, nothing in the *Hatfield* decision convinced me that a meticulously pled Civil RICO claim in a school sex abuse cover-up context could not survive a motion to dismiss.

The *Hatfield* case provided, however, a cautionary note. The legal system was not necessarily the friend of an individual who claimed that a powerful institution facilitated and covered up his sexual abuse. Poor Mr. Hatfield, if his allegations were true (and I have no reason to think otherwise), was sexually molested numerous times over four years, was charged with a felony, lost his job, had his education stalled, and wound up with not a nickel in his pocket for his troubles.

I hesitated before contacting David Hiltbrand because from the outset I was aware that raising the hopes of wounded and emotionally vulnerable men was potentially dangerous and could lead to unintended but draconian consequences. After weighing the pros and cons, however, I chose action over inaction, and forwarded an email to David Hiltbrand in which I complimented David for his courage in telling his story, and suggested a potential Civil RICO litigation approach. I cautioned David, however, that the success or failure of any Civil RICO claim depended on whether he could allege and prove that Poly Prep officials received complaints—other than John Marino's—about Phil Foglietta's sexual assaults of boys but failed to act on them. The devil, or—in the case of Poly Prep—the Blue Devil, was in the details.

Several days after I sent David Hiltbrand my email, in late November 2005, he wrote back, thanked me for my legal input, and suggested that I get in touch with J. Paggioli. David gave me J.'s phone number and I promptly gave J. a call.

The snowball, no bigger than a pebble at the time, had begun its descent down the steep mountain.

CHAPTER TWENTY-NINE

A Puncher's Shot

Above all, don't lie to yourself. The man who lies to himself and listens to his own lie comes to a point that he cannot distinguish the truth within him, or around him, and so loses all respect for himself and for others. And having no respect he ceases to love.

— Fyodor Dostoyevsky, *The Brothers Karamazov*

In 2006, upon J. Paggioli's referral, I met my classmate, Jim Zimmerman, at a New York City restaurant, after not seeing him for twenty-four years.[27] When we went to Poly Prep, Jim and I were friendly acquaintances but certainly not friends. When we squared off on the football field it was all I could do to keep him from knocking me on my butt. Jim was a two-way starter at center and linebacker, a blond-haired, blue-eyed, granite block of a young man, and a co-captain. I was the starting right tackle, mostly by default. We were peers on the gridiron but far from equals.

We were both at least thirty pounds heavier than we had been in high school, and thinning at the top of our heads, but Jim still had that familiar, fierce look of determination and resolve in his steady blue eyes. He looked straight at me, head held high, and told me in painstaking detail how Coach Foglietta had abused him during the early part of our senior year.

I remembered how miserable Jim had been that year. Unlike the prior three years, when Jim sparkled with joy after flattening one over-matched opponent after the other, he skulked and pouted for most of our senior year. He looked and acted as if the last place he wanted to be was on the football field. Jim provided very little of the leadership that was expected from him as one of our captains and best players. In 2006, I finally understood the reason for his black mood that season. I also realized that Phil Foglietta was an absolute maestro at manipulating the emotions, the psyches, and the spirits, of Poly Prep students, even the biggest, strongest, and toughest kids in the school.

By the end of 2007, I had explored every legal option for filing a lawsuit against Poly Prep for facilitating the sexual abuse of J. Paggioli, Jim Zimmerman, and David Hiltbrand, but had determined that winning a lawsuit was extraordinarily difficult, if not impossible. It seemed as if there was no way around the statutes of limitations which had apparently long expired on all possible claims.

My novel Civil RICO theory, which I had shared with David Hiltbrand and J. Paggioli in November 2005, had not gained any traction, as we had not discovered any facts or information that indicated a pattern of racketeering activity because, other than John Marino—who attested that he had told Headmaster William M. Williams and Athletic Director (and Varsity Baseball Coach) Harlow Parker, that he had witnessed Coach Foglietta sexually abusing boys on or near campus (in Foglietta's green Chevy Impala) in the early 1970s—no one had claimed that any school official knew about or had been notified of Foglietta's sexual misconduct.

In 2008, Jim Zimmerman and I thus decided to take an entirely different approach. We developed the idea of forming a charitable organization to help the dozens, if not hundreds, of victims of Phil Foglietta. We dubbed the organization "The White Tower Healing Foundation" in homage to Poly Prep's most famous architectural feature, which can be viewed by anyone crossing the Verrazano Bridge from the Staten Island side into Brooklyn. To get started, we created a website, which provided sexual abuse survivors a forum to share their stories either under their real names or anonymously. And we then persuaded J. Paggioli to manage, oversee, and edit the website on a daily basis.

One of our stated goals was to achieve reconciliation between abuse survivors and the Poly Prep community. On White Tower letterhead, Jim wrote to the school's current headmaster, David Harman, and requested a meeting to voice our concerns and aspirations. We did not threaten litigation. We had no leverage to issue such a threat and, even if we did, our point was to try to obtain reconciliation and avoid confrontation. When Poly Prep failed to respond to our first request for a meeting, Jim sent a second request to David Harman. This time, Harman accepted Jim's invitation, wrote back to him, and scheduled a meeting at the Harvard Club in New York City. But the day before our scheduled meeting, Poly Prep cancelled via email, citing alleged concerns over the make-up of our Board of Directors.

In 2008, Poly Prep thus consciously declined to accept our sincere offer to attempt to achieve reconciliation. Poly officials were likely motivated, at least in part, by their counsel's advice that, from a legal standpoint, Poly Prep had little to worry about abuse incidents that occurred decades ago.

In early 2009, however, a game-changer occurred: Joseph Marino, an early White Tower Director, opened a Facebook page that focused on Coach Foglietta's crimes against children. Bill Jackson, a former Poly Prep student, posted to Joe Marino's Facebook page and claimed that in 1966, Phil Foglietta—in his very first year on staff at Poly Prep—sexually abused him when he (Foglietta) interviewed Jackson about alleged student-on-student sexual misconduct. Bill Jackson also claimed that in 1966, after Foglietta had molested him, he reported the incident directly to Poly's then headmaster, J. Folwell Scull Jr., and athletic director, Harlow Parker. According to Jackson, Scull and Parker told him and his parents that his story was not credible and threatened to expel him if he continued to cause trouble.

Bill, who had dropped out of Poly Prep and struggled with personal demons his entire life, had major trust issues. His parents had credited Poly Prep's version of events over Bill's, and that created a deep rift between mother and father and son that persisted until Bill's parents' deaths. At first, Bill wanted nothing to do with our case. But after Joe introduced him to J. Paggioli, J. began to work diligently to earn Bill's trust and confidence. Eventually, after several months and dozens of communications, J.—both a true believer and fellow survivor—persuaded Bill Jackson to join our case as a plaintiff.

Bill Jackson's alleged report of Foglietta's sexual misconduct to Poly administrators, which occurred within ten years of John Marino's alleged report, permitted us to circumvent the Civil RICO pattern hurdle that required us to plead at least two predicate acts within a ten year period. We now had enough ammunition, maybe, barely, to plead a viable Civil RICO claim, using Poly Prep's false and fraudulent mailings about Foglietta—a known sexual predator—as the necessary predicate acts.

Against the backdrop of this new information, we also had a firm commitment of support from Phil Culhane, a senior partner at Simpson, Thacher & Bartlett, LLP, a prestigious corporate law firm with offices all over the world. Phil had graduated from Poly Prep in 1984 with my brother Sean, two years after Jim, me, and Dennis. He was extremely popular, the president of his class for all four years of high school, and a brilliant student. He also had been repeatedly sexually abused by Coach Foglietta in the late 1970s.

Unlike many survivors who lose their ability to concentrate after suffering sexual assaults, Phil studied with vigor and intensity and obtained exceptional grades. He graduated *magna cum laude* from both Williams College in Massachusetts, one of the best liberal arts colleges in the country, and then New York University Law School. For the last ten years, since about 1998, he had worked as a partner in Simpson's Hong Kong office, specializing in private investment funds.

Despite his considerable professional success, Phil Culhane remained deeply troubled about what had happened to him as a child. When his own son was born, in 2007, the repressed memories of his abuse floated back to the surface of his consciousness. Grotesque images of Foglietta invaded his dreams. And he fretted constantly about being able to protect his son when he had not been able to protect himself.

Phil became livid when he discovered that Foglietta's superiors knew of his crimes against children but did nothing to stop him. Phil Culhane wanted Poly Prep to feel some measure of pain for the considerable pain that it had inflicted upon him and others similarly situated.

In early 2009, I met with Phil Culhane, J. Paggioli, and Jim Zimmerman, at a New York City steakhouse to review our legal options. I told these men that, despite my best efforts, I had been unable to discover a path to a litigation victory. But J., Phil, and Jim were not satisfied with my negative assessment and insisted that there had to be a way, some way, to obtain justice.

At that meeting, Phil Culhane also told me that after he graduated he had made a donation of several thousand dollars to Poly Prep. This was interesting for Civil RICO purposes because that donation may have allowed us to meet the requirement to show a direct loss to "business or property" as a result of the conspiracy at issue.

Phil also told me that he was ready, willing, and able to make a financial commitment to me, if necessary, to support me in a legal battle against Poly Prep's formidable legal team, led by litigation powerhouse O'Melveny & Myers, LLP. This promise meant a great deal to me for, as a sole practitioner, I realized that Poly Prep's lawyers would move aggressively and expeditiously to dismiss our complaint and that to combat that motion I would have to devote a considerable amount of time to the case.

Phil Culhane was true to his word. By December 2012, Phil had contributed about a quarter of a million dollars to my firm. Without Phil Culhane's extraordinarily generous financial support, and frequent practical and wise counsel, I would not have been able to stay in business, much less fight toe-to-toe with Poly Prep's legal army for more than three years.

After Bill Jackson came forward, along with several other brave abuse survivors who wanted to take a puncher's shot at justice, Phil Culhane, Jim Zimmerman, David Hiltbrand, and especially J. Paggioli, implored me to man up, ignore the long odds, pull up my socks, and file a lawsuit against Poly Prep.

On October 9, 2009, I filed a complaint in the U.S. District Court for the Eastern District of New York on behalf of seven plaintiffs against Poly Prep, and several of its principals and employees, for violating Civil RICO.

The case was assigned to Senior District Judge Frederic Block—a known maverick (which, given the novelty and outside-the-box nature of our claims, was a stroke of luck for us)—and Magistrate Judge Cheryl L. Pollak, and assigned Case No. 09-CV-4586. Twenty-nine months after we filed our initial Complaint, we filed a Third Amended Complaint which added five additional plaintiffs (for a total of twelve) and a number of additional claims, including Title IX of the Education Amendments of 1972 (which had been enacted by Congress to prohibit schools that receive federal funds from discriminating against students on the basis of sex).

CHAPTER THIRTY

The Spoils

Ability is the art of getting all the credit for all the home runs somebody else hits.

— Casey Stengel

Except on those rare occasions when a batter gets a hit to end the game, a ballplayer's chance to be a hero is in large part not in his control. His achievement: a home run, a diving catch, a key strikeout, will be diminished in memory if his opponents find a way to beat his team. The converse is also true: if a player's achievement stands up and leads to victory, it will be elevated in memory, in legend.

A good example of this is the playoff game on October 2, 1978 between the New York Yankees and Boston Red Sox. Most people remember that the game was won by Bucky Dent, who—in New England—has a distinct middle name that rhymes with "trucking." Many baseball fans know that Bucky Dent poked his three run homer over the Green Monster in the top of the seventh inning. But most people forget that in that same inning Thurman Munson doubled to deep center to drive in Mickey Rivers, who had walked. Or that Reggie Jackson homered off Bob Stanley (who would resurface again in the 1986 World Series) to lead off the eighth inning.

And most people don't remember that in the bottom of the ninth, Yankees' closer, Rich "Goose" Gossage—who had surrendered two runs in the previous inning—walked Rick Burleson with one out and then gave up a line single to right to Jerry Remy. The Red Sox had the tying run on second, and the winning run on first, with one out and two future Hall of Famers—Jim Rice and Carl Yastrzemski—coming up to bat.

Rice hit a flyball to deep right field, which permitted Burleson to tag and move to third. So it was left to Yastrzemski, the Sox's aging, longtime star, to try and drive in the Red Sox's fifth run and tie the game.

Leading off the second inning, Yaz had given the Red Sox the lead with a home run against Ron Guidry, the Yankees' ace—who finished 1978 with the remarkable record of twenty-five wins and three losses. Yaz had also singled sharply to center against Gossage in the bottom of the eighth to pull the Red Sox within one run of the Yankees. But, in the bottom of the ninth, Yaz popped up an outside fastball to Graig Nettles, who hugged the third base line and caught the ball to the side of his left shoulder for the final out. And Bucky Dent became a legend.

The best example of a player who should have become a hero, but did not, is Dave Henderson of the 1986 Boston Red Sox. In the deciding Game Five of the American League Championship Series between the Red Sox and California Angels, Henderson hit a two run homer to deep left field off Donnie Moore with two outs in the top of the ninth inning and the Red Sox trailing by a run. In the bottom of the ninth, the Angels came back and tied the game by scratching out a run against Red Sox relievers Bob Stanley (yes, him again) and Steve Crawford.

The Angels also loaded the bases that inning with only one out but could not push across the game-winning run, as Doug DeCinces popped out to short right field and Bobby Grich lined back to the pitcher. Dave Henderson, for good measure, then drove in the game-winning run in the top of the eleventh inning with a sacrifice fly to center field which scored Don Baylor (who had reached base by getting plunked by the Angels' star-crossed reliever, Donnie Moore).

When the Red Sox traveled to New York in the World Series against the Mets, Dave Henderson still had some magic in his bat. With the Sox leading the Series three games to two, and Game Six tied at three after regulation, Henderson led off the top of the tenth inning with a line drive, a frozen rope, far over the left field fence, off Mets' pitcher Rick Aguilera. Later that inning, the Red Sox added an insurance run with a double to left center by Wade Boggs (another future Hall of Famer) and a single up the middle by Marty Barrett.

Then the bottom of the tenth unfolded; John McNamara kept Dave Stapleton on the bench; Calvin Schiraldi and Bob Stanley imploded; Rich Gedman failed to catch an inside pitch; and Bill Buckner let a dribbler go through his legs. Dave Henderson, who would likely have been canonized in Boston had the Red Sox hung on to win, faded into the historical woodwork. Hondo was not tabbed with an expletive for a middle name by New York fans. And, of course, Henderson had absolutely nothing to do with the Red Sox's loss of Game Six. He was just an unfortunate victim of circumstances which diminished his own achievements, not in deed but in memory.

Bucky Dent is immortalized. Dave Henderson—who died from a heart attack (at just fifty-seven) on December 27, 2015—is largely forgotten. Their respective statuses and reputations derive almost entirely from the actions of other people. Who said life, or baseball, was fair? And who thinks for a second that the credit for high achievement is always properly distributed?

John Joseph "J." Paggioli is the unsung hero of the *Zimmerman v. Poly Prep* case. He started a revolution in New York State, which affected not just students from Poly Prep and Horace Mann, but students of many other schools in the New York metropolitan area. In April 2004, when J. first filed suit against Poly Prep, he had no co-plaintiffs, no factual corroboration of his claims, no viable legal theory for winning his case, and no chance in hell of getting justice against Poly Prep and Phil Foglietta's individual facilitators and enablers. What he did have were an extraordinary amount of guts and courage—he was not afraid to publicly proclaim that he had been repeatedly sexually assaulted as a child—and the deep conviction that Foglietta—the school's golden goose—could not have been so brazen and prolific in his abuse unless Poly Prep officials operated under a "see no evil, hear no evil" policy when it came to Foglietta's extracurricular activities.

When we filed suit against Poly Prep in October 2009, J., by virtue of his knowledge and contributions to the cause, should have been the lead, first-named plaintiff. But when I told him that the group was better served with Jim Zimmerman as the first-named plaintiff, primarily because Jim was extremely well-liked and respected by many in the Poly Prep community, J. swallowed his pride and assented to that decision.

Once the lawsuit began, J. was relentless in discovering new information, other victims, additional plaintiffs, helpful documents, and even—on several occasions—legal theories or strategies. I recognized that J. was a force of nature and, frequently, sat back and set him in motion. The results, the new and helpful information, usually followed shortly thereafter.

J. devised a brilliant strategy and persuaded me to use it as often as I could. We called it "Bizzaro Legal World," and the idea was that we would try to figure out what Poly Prep and its counsel, Jeffrey Kohn of O'Melveny & Myers, LLP, wanted us to do, and then we would do the exact opposite. The best example of this was our pursuit of fraud upon the court sanctions against Poly Prep and its lawyers.

A fraud upon the court occurs only when a party can establish that his litigation adversary has "set in motion some unconscionable scheme calculated to interfere with the judicial system's ability to impartially adjudicate a matter by ... unfairly hampering the presentation of the opposing party's claim or defense." [28] Unlike garden-variety fraud, or an isolated instance of perjury, the essence of fraud upon the court—an attempt by a party to defile the court itself—is "when a party lies to the court and his adversary intentionally, repeatedly, and about issues that are central to the truth-finding process." [29]

When Jeffrey Kohn made it clear that he did not want us to pursue a fraud on the court theory—and warned us that we were on flimsy legal and ethical ground if we did so—we made sure to quickly file a motion to the Court seeking fraud upon the court sanctions (which included, possibly, a default judgment) against Poly Prep.

We argued that Poly Prep's mantra—that no one at Poly Prep knew of Phil Foglietta's sexual misconduct until 1991—which was consistently parroted by Poly Prep administrators, faculty members, and lawyers in the *Zimmerman* litigation, was a blatant falsehood. This "Big Lie" was so egregious, we claimed, that it arose to a fraud upon the court.

On the evening of Thursday, August 26, 2010, I called my dad at about 7:00 p.m. and told him that I would not be able to join him at the Barclay's PGA Golf Tournament the next day (that year the PGA had moved the tournament from its traditional site at the Westchester Country Club in Harrison, New York to the Ridgewood Country Club in Paramus, New Jersey). This was a father-son tradition, as my father and I had enjoyed Friday rounds at the Barclay's Tournament for three of the last five years. I told my dad that I was expecting Poly Prep's fraud upon the court motion opposition papers the next day, and needed to start working right away on plaintiffs' reply brief. My father was not at all upset about the eleventh hour cancellation (which surprised me) and told me that he would skip the tournament and instead golf with his friends at the Philip J. Rotella Golf Course (in Thiells, New York) the next morning.

We then talked for a few minutes about the Poly Prep case. I asked my dad point-blank if he had any problem with me suing my alma mater.

"It depends on if they knew, Kevin. If they knew, the hell with them. Do what you need to do."

"They knew, Dad. I'm sure of that. The problem with this crazy law is that it might not matter. There are a helluva lot of hoops that we need to jump through."

"Well, if they knew, I'm behind you all the way, Kevin. Go get 'em. Keep fighting," my father said right before he hung up the phone.

The next day, August 27, 2010, I received Poly Prep's motion opposition papers some time mid-morning. As I was reviewing these papers, in which Poly Prep issued a blanket denial of each and every allegation that we had made, I received a phone call from an Emergency Medical Technician who advised me that my father had collapsed at the Philip J. Rotella Golf Course and was being rushed to Good Samaritan Hospital in Suffern, New York.

By the time I arrived at Good Samaritan, twenty minutes later, it was too late. My father had died. Although we initially thought Dad had died from a heart attack, we found out later that a diabetic stroke, not a heart attack, had felled him. He was probably gone the moment he collapsed to the ground just outside the Golf Course's café. My father lived seventy years and twenty days. He was truly one of a kind.

On June 5, 2012, Magistrate Judge Cheryl L. Pollak, in addressing the *Zimmerman* plaintiffs' second fraud upon the court motion, held that an evidentiary hearing was necessary to resolve whether the Poly Prep defendants engaged in fraud on the court or a vigorous, legally acceptable, defense.[30]

Several of Judge Pollak's sons had recently graduated from New York City prep schools. She was obviously appalled by Poly Prep's conduct and a stalwart proponent of plaintiffs' novel but colorable legal theories throughout the litigation. Judge Pollak, at every turn, fought for justice in this case. She fought for the plaintiffs. She recognized that the law needed to provide these men, wounded grievously as defenseless children, with some relief, some remedy.

Judge Pollak is a woman, a mother, a citizen, first, and a judge second. And that makes her a great judge. Judge Pollak has an abiding conviction that the law that she serves is meant to help, not hurt, people, and to right, not perpetuate, wrongs. Too many of her judicial brethren, far too many, fail to embrace that precept as a guiding principle.

In her June 5, 2012 Order, Judge Pollak scheduled an evidentiary hearing on the fraud upon the court issue for July 19, 2012. She certainly seemed ready to hold Poly Prep accountable for its acts and omissions. My twelve clients were downright ecstatic that they were about to get a peek at Lady Justice in all her glory.

But their euphoria was short-lived. Just fifteen days later, on June 20, 2012, Judge Block conducted oral argument on Poly Prep's motion to dismiss, stated that "plaintiffs have a tough road," and gave every indication that he would likely soon grant Poly Prep's motion to dismiss *all* of plaintiffs' claims. He also notified counsel and the parties that the fraud upon the court hearing scheduled for July 19th by Judge Pollak would be adjourned until after he issued a decision on Poly Prep's motion to dismiss.

As I walked out of the federal courthouse that afternoon with Ed Flanders, my co-counsel from Pillsbury Winthrop Shaw Pittman LLP, Jim Zimmerman, and two "John Doe" plaintiffs, I was disheartened to see the shell-shocked looks on my clients' faces. Each looked as if he had been conked on the head with a baseball bat. Each whispered a few perfunctory words of thanks, and—crestfallen and disconsolate—walked out of the courthouse as fast as possible. There was no mistaking Judge Block's intentions: he was about to dismiss the case. Poly Prep was about to win and the plaintiffs were about to lose. Again.

I tried to appeal to Judge Pollak because I knew that she had a vast reservoir of empathy for my clients and their plights. She had scheduled a conference on an application made by Poly Prep for June 22, 2012. But when I arrived at this conference and began to argue about the unfairness of Judge Block's edict to push aside the fraud upon the court evidentiary hearing, Judge Pollak made it clear that there was nothing she could do. Judge Block was the district judge, and she, Judge Pollak, was the magistrate. She was outranked and I was, it seemed for the moment, poleaxed.

Judge Block's June 20, 2012 conference, which I nicknamed the "De-Blockal," had driven my clients away from the courthouse. On June 22, 2012, for the first time in the case, Jim Zimmerman and his fellow plaintiffs were not in attendance at a court proceeding. But I was glad that they were not there to see Judge Pollak—their stalwart judicial advocate—throw up her hands in obvious frustration and judicial impotence.

After the conference before Judge Pollak, as I walked across the park adjacent to the Cadman Plaza Courthouse with Michael O'Keeffe, a reporter for the *New York Daily News,* I kept picturing the anguished faces of Jim Zimmerman and his co-plaintiffs. What kind of havoc had I wreaked?

I had put these men through an emotional roller-coaster, only for them to be decimated in the end by a judicial wringer. I had also crossed the line of objectivity and lawyerly detachment. These men were not just my clients anymore; they were my friends. It was now far beyond "personal." The downward spiral of this case was cutting me to ribbons. I could only imagine what it was doing to them.

Michael O'Keeffe accepted my lunch invitation and sat down across from me in a booth at the Greek diner across the street from the courthouse. Michael published more than twenty articles about the Poly Prep case in the *Daily News.* His critical and, at times, scathing, commentary on the judicial proceedings kept us in the public eye. His unrelenting coverage of the case—usually with the accurate and fair-minded slant that plaintiffs deserved their day in court and Poly Prep deserved condemnation for its conduct—also likely put some pressure on Judge Block to not summarily dismiss the case.

On this day, though, Michael could tell by my hollow eyes that, for the first time, I viewed the Poly Prep case as a lost cause, a professional and personal disaster. But my defeatism did not last too long. As we munched on our sandwiches, I vented about how Judge Block's postponement of the fraud upon the court hearing was unprecedented in American jurisprudence.

"I've researched this issue, Mike, and I'm telling you that—as far as I can tell—no district judge has ever overruled a magistrate who had scheduled an evidentiary hearing on a fraud upon the court motion. Ever. Not in any federal court, not in any state, not in the whole damn country. Not once."

"That's interesting," Michael said. "Can I write about that?"

"I wish you would," I replied.

At that moment, I was able to see yet another glimmer of hope. All was not lost; we still had good people fighting for us. Michael O'Keeffe honored his word. He published not one, but two, articles about Poly Prep's alleged fraud upon the court. I am convinced that Michael O'Keeffe's tenacious reporting was instrumental in helping the *Zimmerman* plaintiffs survive Poly Prep's motion to dismiss and eventually navigate their way to a settlement.

On August 28, 2012, two years and one day after my father died, District Judge Frederic Block issued a Memorandum and Order which denied the bulk of Poly Prep's motion to dismiss the *Zimmerman* plaintiffs' Third Amended Complaint.[31] Judge Block ruled that plaintiffs had plausibly alleged that Poly Prep engaged in an affirmative course of conduct during the period of limitations to deceive the plaintiffs into believing that they had no claims against Poly Prep despite the school's knowledge that Foglietta had sexually abused boys at Poly Prep. "[T]hat deceitful conduct . . . might plausibly have led [the plaintiffs] to falsely believe that Poly Prep was unaware of Foglietta's misconduct and could not be liable for negligent retention or supervision."[32]

Judge Block ordered discovery to proceed and also ordered a hearing, after discovery, to determine if plaintiffs could prove that Poly Prep's myriad statements about Foglietta's "lily white reputation were false and made with knowledge of their falsity," that the plaintiffs had justifiably relied on the school's misrepresentations and deceitful conduct in not bringing suit during the limitations period, and that the plaintiffs had acted with due diligence in bringing their suit within a reasonable period of time after they learned of Poly Prep's misconduct.[33]

Judge Block also tackled the Civil RICO issue and determined that Phil Culhane and Phil Henningsen, a former star quarterback and baseball player at Poly Prep who had joined the lawsuit (first as a John Doe plaintiff and then under his true name)—and was a voice of reason and a calming influence on many of his fellow plaintiffs—, had both stated viable Civil RICO claims against certain individual defendants because their post-graduation donations to Poly Prep permitted them to adequately allege that they suffered a cognizable injury caused by violations of the RICO statute.[34]

To my knowledge, this is the first and only time in American history that Civil RICO has been successfully pled in a school sex abuse cover-up context.

During a meeting in Judge Block's chambers about a year after the Poly Prep case ended, Judge Block informed me that his clerk's first draft of the decision recommended a complete dismissal of all the *Zimmerman* plaintiffs' claims. He then told me that he decided not to dismiss the case because Judge Pollak argued vehemently and passionately that plaintiffs' claims were plausible. I credit Judge Block for having enough of an open mind to heed the wise and compassionate advice of his magistrate. And, although Judge Block himself may not believe this, he was right on the law. His decision to deny Poly Prep's motion to dismiss was both righteous and right.

On September 14, 2012, I appeared before Judge Block at the federal court in Cadman Plaza (in Brooklyn) with the expectation that the Court would schedule an evidentiary hearing, as ordered by Judge Pollak, on the fraud upon the court issue, and schedule a subsequent evidentiary hearing, as ordered by Judge Block, on the equitable estoppel issue (i.e., whether plaintiffs could circumvent the applicable statutes of limitations because of Poly Prep's alleged post-abuse misconduct).

A fraud upon the court hearing would have permitted us to examine the nine Poly Prep teachers, former teachers, administrators, and former administrators, who testified categorically during their depositions that they had no inkling of Foglietta's penchant to sexually assault children until 1991 (when Headmaster Williams received David Hiltbrand's letter). I planned to prove that many of these claims were false—and that numerous Poly officials had received complaints or information about Foglietta's sexual misconduct from the inception of his tenure at the school (1966) until his departure (in 1991).

The strongest part of our case, by far, was Poly Prep's alleged fraud, and that issue also had the side benefit of overlapping with the substantive legal elements that we needed to prove in order to obtain a verdict for plaintiffs. At the September 14, 2012 hearing, however, Judge Block was again contemptuous of our fraud upon the court argument, and he issued an indefinite stay of the fraud upon the court hearing. Judge Block made clear that, unlike his own magistrate judge, he did not take our fraud upon the court allegations seriously. When I tried to argue the issue, he told me to sit down and "stop showing off" for my clients. Judge Block would address our fraud claim when, and only when, he felt like doing so. Which, he implied, was probably going to be never.

With our strongest ammunition removed from our litigation guns, we now had no leverage to negotiate a *fair* settlement with Poly Prep. But, in spite of Judge Block's removal of the fraud upon the court threat, Poly Prep—for reasons I do not fully understand—still decided to pursue a serious settlement dialogue. After lengthy and contentious negotiations, with both monetary and non-monetary issues in play, the *Zimmerman* plaintiffs reached a settlement with Poly Prep in the last week of December 2012.

There is no doubt that J. Paggioli has not received the credit he deserves. Without his herculean efforts at all phases of the litigation, the *Zimmerman* plaintiffs would not have survived Poly Prep's motion to dismiss and Poly would not have settled the case. The converse, of course, is also true. Without the other eleven plaintiffs and their contributions, J. would never have survived a motion to dismiss.

While J. is at times quite difficult, I understand—at least to some extent—the provenance of his frequent anger and easily triggered rage. J's childhood innocence was stolen from him by craven school administrators who placed Poly's reputation over the well-being of many of its wounded, vulnerable sons, including John Joseph Paggioli.

While J.'s anger is sometimes self-destructive and prevents him from finding the peace that he has earned, I must acknowledge that his rage may have been the fuel that permitted him and his co-plaintiffs to obtain some measure of justice against Poly Prep. Without J.'s anger, his rage, his wrath, it would have been quite difficult for us to marshal the energy and power to fight our litigation foes with the necessary ferocity, perseverance, and resolve.

J.'s rage at Poly Prep is—for numerous reasons—entirely justified. But now, three years after the Poly Prep settlement, I can only hope that J. can take his anger and transform it into a more positive kind of energy—one that will lead him to joy and happiness. He deserves, after all he has endured, and after all he has contributed, to know that feeling, that emotion.

This book does not pretend to tell the full story of the *Zimmerman v. Poly Prep* litigation. I am not the appropriate person to tell the full story of that case. My twelve clients, who summoned the courage to stand up and demand justice, and who refused to let Phil Foglietta's destruction of their childhood innocence deter them from obtaining some measure of truth and accountability from the school that failed to protect them, are better suited to tell this complex, fascinating, and deeply disturbing tale. I hope, at some point, one or more of them does so.

CHAPTER THIRTY-ONE

Perverted Justice

There is no crueler tyranny than that which is perpetuated under the shield of law and in the name of justice.

— Charles de Montesquieu

On a hot, sticky day in August 2013, I arrived at the Daniel P. Moynihan Federal Courthouse in downtown Manhattan, at about 2:30 p.m. My paralegal, Tom Butterworth, a student at Fordham University, was with me. We were there for our first appearance in the venerable United States District Court for the Southern District of New York, before the Honorable John G. Koeltl, in the matter of *Mordechai Twersky, et al. v. Yeshiva University, et al.,*[35] a school sex abuse cover-up case.

Our initial Complaint, filed on behalf of nineteen plaintiffs, all former students at the prestigious Marsha Stern Talmudical Academy-Yeshiva University High School for Boys ("YUHS"), consisted of five hundred and sixty-four paragraphs which alleged that my clients had been sexually assaulted by two rabbis during their tenure as students at YUHS (located on Amsterdam Avenue in Manhattan) in the 70s and 80s. The rabbis, George Finkelstein and Macy Gordon, were revered authority figures, a Principal and Judaic Studies teacher, respectively, at the school.

The school's multi-decade cover-up had finally been exposed in December 2012 when Paul Berger, a reporter for the *Jewish Daily Forward*, knocked on the door of Dr. Rabbi Norman Lamm's Manhattan apartment, asked some questions, and received some surprisingly straight answers.

Lamm, who was Yeshiva University's then chancellor and former president, told Berger that "[i]f it was an open-and-shut case [of abuse], I just let the [staff member] go quietly. It was not our intention or position to destroy a person without further inquiry."[36]

The cover-up allegations in the Complaint were both voluminous and horrendous. We alleged that at least fourteen school officials had received at least twenty-two separate sexual abuse complaints about Finkelstein and/or Gordon, but acted with callous indifference to all of these complaints. No law enforcement officials were contacted. No students (or their parents) were warned about these predator rabbis. No punitive action of any kind was taken by Yeshiva University, which governed YUHS and was in charge of disciplining (and hiring and firing) YUHS employees. Yeshiva University instead made the conscious, craven decision to continue to employ Finkelstein and Gordon and leave them free to sexually assault scores of innocent, unsuspecting boys.[37] The school decided to protect its name and reputation to the considerable lifelong detriment of its students. The conduct of Yeshiva University's administrators, as our one hundred and fifty page Complaint practically screamed, was unconscionable.

I had forgotten to bring several documents to the Court which I might have needed to reference during our hearing, so I called my secretary, Sally, and had her email me the documents to my phone. When I passed through the Court's security checkpoint I told the court officer that I needed to bring my phone to the courtroom.

"No problem, counselor. But you need to get the Judge's permission. Just have the Judge's clerk call down here from chambers with the Judge's consent—and we'll let you have your phone."

As Tom and I were a half hour early for the conference, we had time to take care of this administrative detail. So we took an elevator to the 10th Floor and proceeded to Judge Koeltl's chambers. When we were buzzed in we were met by an attractive, well-dressed female staffer. After we explained our request, she smiled brightly and went in to see the Judge. As we waited, I admired the outer part of Judge Koeltl's chambers. The carpet was bright and fresh; the furniture looked new and polished; and there was not a scrap of paper out of place.

Fifteen minutes later the woman staffer emerged from Judge Koeltl's inner chamber. Her smile was replaced by a frown.

"I'm sorry. There is nothing we can do. Judge Koeltl says that he has no authority to permit you to bring a phone into his courtroom."

After we left the chambers, I shot Tom a hard glare.

"That's a real asshole move."

Tom nodded. "Yea, the security guard made it seem like your request was no big deal. Like it was routine."

"That's a bad freaking omen," I said, as we marched toward the courtroom. "A bad freaking omen."

Twenty minutes later, we were standing at the front table in Judge Koeltl's courtroom. He sat placidly in his black robe, a pleasant enough looking man in his late-sixties, about to hear an important case about a school's recently exposed multi-decade cover-up of the sexual abuse of many of its students. Judge Koeltl asked me to tell him about the case.

"Your Honor, we would like to emphasize to the Court, respectfully, that this is not a, quote unquote, old sex abuse case. What this is is a newly discovered school cover-up sex abuse case, and the difference is very distinct.

"This is a case in which we are alleging that from 1971 through 1991, when the principal at issue, George Finkelstein, was terminated from the school, Yeshiva University and Yeshiva University High School for Boys, allowed dozens of its students to be sexually abused in the most heinous of ways by two faculty members and administrators, George Finkelstein and Macy Gordon, respectively ...[38]

"The most egregious example of abuse was the sodomization of one of my clients, John Doe 2, with a tooth brush by Macy Gordon. That individual was so traumatized by the event that he tried to kill himself thereafter in his dormitory room. Several weeks later he and his father, who is a respected member of the community, spoke to senior administrator Israel Miller at [Yeshiva University] and told him in graphic detail horrible incident after horrible incident of what happened to him. Remarkably, nothing was done to Macy Gordon for another four years. He stayed there until 1984. And in the interim, at least one other individual, John Doe 16, was sexually abused by the same man six months or so after Macy Gordon's vicious sexual assault was reported to Yeshiva University." [39]

I then asked the Court for the right to take discovery, which would permit me to obtain relevant documents in the defendants' possession and take depositions of various individuals with knowledge of plaintiffs' claims. The ability to take discovery was critical to plaintiffs' success because the details of Yeshiva University's cover-up and conspiracy were in Yeshiva University's sole possession.

I pressed the issue.

"[A] motion for a stay [of discovery] must be supported by a substantial argument for dismissal. In other words, there must be a strong showing that plaintiff's claim is unmeritorious ... [T]hese facts show anything but. This case has extreme merit." [40]

Judge Koeltl did not budge. "OK. If the motion to dismiss should be denied because you have alleged enough to survive a motion to dismiss, then, of course, discovery goes forward. The issue is complaints are not filed in order to get discovery. You have to allege sufficient facts to survive a motion to dismiss, not factual allegations to state a claim." [41]

The die had been cast. In a Hail Mary pitch, I referenced Yeshiva University's own investigation of abuse issues in which the school's investigative team interviewed more than a hundred people about the sexual abuse of boys by faculty and staff at YUHS (and other schools affiliated with Yeshiva University) and Yeshiva University's response to various abuse complaints and allegations.

"You're basically having plaintiffs tie one hand behind their backs because much of the information is in the hands of the defendants. I know that [Yeshiva University has] conducted a seven month investigation independently, talked to dozens, if not hundreds, of individuals with respect to issues pertaining to notice of abuse and the school's response to notice. It would be unfair and prejudicial to the plaintiffs to go forward and have our plaintiffs put in legal jeopardy on a motion to dismiss without that information being in our possession."

My argument went nowhere. Judge Koeltl, after hearing from Yeshiva University's counsel, set a briefing schedule for defendants' motion to dismiss and denied plaintiffs' request for pre-motion discovery. He then discussed page length limits.

"If the complaint is one hundred and fifty pages, I will give you thirty-five, thirty-five, and fifteen, for the motion to dismiss, the response and the reply. Please don't adjust the font, the margins, double space the footnotes. Don't adjust the type size. Don't make me read the brief with a magnifying glass. The brief is meant to be persuasive. If I can't read it, it's not persuasive. Have I missed any other techniques?" [42]

I attempted to inject some levity into the proceeding. "I assume single space is out of the question?" [43]

Judge Koeltl failed to respond to my attempt at humor. "Regular spacing, thank you," he replied in a dull monotone. [44]

Tom and I walked back to my car, which I had parked in a lot on Duane Street. We took a right turn onto Chambers Street and another onto the West Side Highway. As we traveled north up the Henry Hudson Parkway, over the George Washington Bridge, and again north on the Palisades Parkway, we assessed the conference and the future of our case.

At first we tried to talk ourselves into believing that it was not that bad, that this judge would give us a fair shake, but the more we drove the less sanguine we became about our prospects for victory.

"Tell me this, Tom, did this judge express one word of outrage for the conduct of Yeshiva or one iota of sympathy for the pain suffered by the plaintiffs?"

"Come to think of it, no on either count," Tom replied.

"And that's all we really need to know. This case is about children being sodomized and sexually assaulted for decades. And the school's top officials knew about this conduct all along. And this judge *still* can't manage to muster even the slightest bit of anger or outrage. He acted like this was a run-of-the-mill securities litigation, not a case where a school cravenly permitted two assholes predators to sexually abuse dozens of kids for thirty years!

"And to not let us have discovery. What a fucking joke. He's not letting us have discovery because he has no intention of letting this case get to first base. He knows discovery will bury the school, so he'll make sure that won't happen. This case is dead on arrival, Tom. D.O.A."

Tom was silent for a moment and then looked at me and nodded grimly. "I hate to agree with you, Kevin, but I think you're one hundred percent right. I think we're totally screwed."

Over the next few weeks, fifteen plaintiffs joined the lawsuit (for a total of thirty-four), and all alleged that they had been sexually abused by George Finkelstein, Macy Gordon, or both. Several of them claimed that they had attempted suicide as a direct result of their abuse by these "rabbis." And more than a half dozen plaintiffs claimed that they had reported their sexual assaults to school officials, all of whom responded with yawns of indifference or snarled threats of retaliation if the complainants were to press forward with their allegations.

But none of this mattered. None of the eight hundred and ninety-seven allegations or the two hundred and fifty-eight pages in the Amended Complaint mattered. We were dismissed on timeliness grounds, ultimately, on an argument that Yeshiva University not only failed to make, but vehemently argued against.

The key legal issue in this case was when did the three-year statute of limitations start to run on plaintiffs' Title IX claims. I argued that the United States Supreme Court made this issue crystal clear: a statute of limitations on a federal claim accrues (begins to run) when a plaintiff knows or has reason to know of the injury that is the basis of his claim.[45] We alleged that the *Twersky* plaintiffs did not know (and could not have known) of the actionable Title IX injury—Yeshiva University's deliberate indifference to its administrators' actual knowledge of sexual abuse at YUHS—until December 2012, when Paul Berger published his expose of Yeshiva University's sex abuse cover-up in the *Jewish Daily Forward.*

Yeshiva University, through its attorneys, Greenberg Traurig, LLP, argued *exclusively* that plaintiffs' claims accrued at the time each plaintiff was sexually assaulted and that the deliberate indifference issue was irrelevant to accrual. Yeshiva University thus waved a symbolic white flag in the event the Court were to find that my proposed accrual standard was correct, as it deliberately chose to not make the argument, in any way, shape, or form, that any of the plaintiffs could have or would have discovered Yeshiva University administrators' deliberate indifference to sexual abuse at YUHS at any time earlier than December 2012.

Judge Koeltl, in his dismissal decision, seemed to take Yeshiva University's side on this issue but was deliberately and frustratingly obtuse.[46] On appeal, the Second Circuit agreed with me that the proper accrual trigger was the dates plaintiffs knew or should have known of Yeshiva University's deliberate indifference to sexual abuse at YUHS.[47]

Again, that finding should have mandated a denial of Yeshiva University's motion to dismiss because the school had put all of its timeliness eggs in the wrongheaded basket that the statute of limitations began to run after each plaintiff was sexually abused—and had thus not bothered to make *any* argument that my clients knew or should have known of the actionable deliberate indifference of Yeshiva University administrators at any time earlier than the time plaintiffs stated in their complaint.

In a remarkable display of judicial overreach, however, the Second Circuit panel affirmed Judge Koeltl's dismissal on the basis that plaintiffs somehow should have known of Yeshiva University's deliberate indifference to sex abuse at YUHS by the time they left the school.[48] That conclusion ignored that Yeshiva University's prolonged, successful, and admitted cover-up made it impossible for any plaintiff to have discovered Yeshiva University administrators' deliberate indifference to sex abuse at YUHS prior to his own assaults.

The Second Circuit panel's decision also violated the principle of party presentation—a sacrosanct rule that parties, not judges, must develop facts and make legal arguments, and that judges must remain as neutral arbiters and *not* act as de facto attorneys for any party in an ongoing litigation. Judges must judge and lawyers must present facts and arguments. Otherwise, attorneys and parties will have no fair opportunity to rebut the arguments and theories crafted and propounded not by the parties and their counsel, but by the judges. And chaos and inequity will reign.

In *Twersky*, the Second Circuit panel concluded that post-abuse sexual assault complaints made to school officials by a minority of plaintiffs, and Yeshiva University's continued retention of the two employees complained about, were sufficient to establish that *all* of the plaintiffs knew or should have known of Yeshiva University's actionable deliberate indifference to sex abuse at YUHS by the time the plaintiffs left the high school.[49] This conclusion, manufactured by the panel from thin air as opposed to any argument made by Yeshiva University itself, violated the Supreme Court rule that for a school to be liable to a student under Title IX, its deliberate indifference *must—not maybe, not possibly, but must*—directly cause students to "undergo harassment" (i.e., sex abuse) or make them "vulnerable to it."[50]

The direct and proximate cause element of Title IX likewise provides that a student's knowledge of a school's indifference to his complaints to school officials *after* his own assault occurred is meaningless to the issue of whether that student could plausibly allege that a school's deliberate indifference *caused* or facilitated his own sexual assault and thus violated Title IX. The Second Circuit panel's case-ending finding of fact—that plaintiffs knew or should have known of Yeshiva University's actionable deliberate indifference by the time they left YUHS—thus cannot be squared with the Supreme Court's unequivocal rule that for a Title IX plaintiff to succeed in a school sex abuse cover-up case, he *must* plead and prove that his school's officials acted with deliberate indifference prior to his own assault.[51]

The *Twersky* case demonstrates why the principle of party presentation should be—and, with extraordinarily rare exceptions, almost always is—followed by federal courts. Had Yeshiva University, rather than the Second Circuit panel, argued that post-abuse complaints by nine plaintiffs were sufficient to establish that all thirty-four plaintiffs had the requisite knowledge of Yeshiva University's deliberate indifference while plaintiffs were still attending YUHS, plaintiffs would have been able to brief the issue and explain to the Court, the ultimate decider, that such an argument was frivolous, contrary to the facts in the record, and, most critically, directly antithetical to the Supreme Court's unequivocal pronouncement on that precise issue.[52] The Second Circuit panel, instead, both fabricated a preposterous conclusion *and* denied plaintiffs any fair opportunity to demonstrate its gross legal and factual deficiencies.

The *Twersky* case thus featured the most egregious display of judicial bias and abuse of authority that I have ever witnessed in my twenty-five-year career as an attorney. It was a railroad job to beat all railroad jobs.

I recognize that many defenders of Yeshiva University and the judges that I take to task in this book will argue that my assessment is nothing more than sour grapes from an unsuccessful litigant. These people will be spectacularly wrong and ill-informed. A careful and thorough review of the record will reveal this case for what it is: an ugly, preposterous, intellectually dishonest, and indefensible rape of justice.

My thirty-four clients all attended YUHS expecting to receive an education rooted in the best Jewish traditions, but instead were molested or sodomized by one or two employees of Yeshiva University whom the school's top administrators *knew* were sexual predators who had previously abused numerous students. Then, Yeshiva University's prolonged and successful cover-up and conspiracy of silence (on behalf of which school administrators continued to bestow many honors and accolades upon the two men whom they *knew* were serial child molesters) forced these wounded boys to drag the resulting emotional baggage around their necks, like chains of degradation which grew heavier upon every step, for decades. These decent, brave, and honorable men—who found the strength to shed their chains and demand accountability from the school that betrayed them—deserved far better than the judicial farce, the unfunny clown show, that was inflicted upon them by two of the most venerable courts in the United States.

Our initial assessment of Judge Koeltl's intention to dismiss—facts or law be damned—could not have been more accurate. Judge Koeltl and his friends on the Second Circuit who affirmed his dismissal have perverted justice in this case.

Rape of justice. Perverted justice. The reviolation of sexual abuse victims through the use of judicial machinery. I do not use these words lightly. But if the shoe fits . . .

CHAPTER THIRTY-TWO

Sheep

The great creative individual ... is capable of more wisdom and virtue than collective man ever can be.

— John Stuart Mill

The ritual, believed to have begun in Wrigley Field, now infects practically every Major League stadium. A batter for the visiting team slugs a home run into the bleachers or outfield seats. After a scrum, a clean catch, or a virtual pinball game, a lucky fan winds up with the baseball in his hands. Tightly stitched, cowhide leather rubbed in mud from the New Jersey side of the Delaware River, this baseball is a special prize. A home run ball hit in a Major League game.

But then the chorus of the home crowd begins. Often just a slow and steady murmur, but, sometimes, allowed to fester, a series of catcalls or a cacophony of boos. Throw it back! More often than not, the lucky fan throws the ball back without much, if any, prompting. Sometimes, aware of the value, sentimental or otherwise, of the prize catch, the chorus of boos must increase in volume ... but, inevitably, the lottery winner, catcher of the home run ball, acquiesces to the will of the mob and heaves the baseball back onto the field, and, if he has a half-way decent arm, toward the infield.

Over the last ten years—with the exception of an industrious Cubs fan who, in 2014, pulled a classic bait and switch and sacrificed to Wrigley Field an old ball he had hidden in his pocket—I don't remember seeing any home run balls hit by members of the away team not return to the field. I think this is a disturbing practice for I bet that nine out of ten people who catch a home run ball would love to keep it, even if a player on the visiting team—not the beloved home squad—launched it into the stands. But the ball catchers become sheep, unable to stand up to the mob, unable to think for themselves, unable to stand up and fight for their own desires.

Do not these stadium patrons, these sheep, represent a microcosm of our society as a whole?

It is high time for us to start thinking, once again, for ourselves.

We need to put our own individual values, goals, needs, and desires above the whim and demand of the mob, the worshipped collective, the washed and unwashed masses. Only then, when we assert our individual will—when we insist on keeping that home run ball hit by a visiting team player—will we be truly free.

"Home of the free and land of the brave."

We hear these words before every Major League ballgame.

Are they an empty platitude or words to live by?

The answer is entirely up to us.

CHAPTER THIRTY-THREE

Lost Boys

As far as we can discern, the sole purpose of human existence is to kindle a light in the darkness of mere being. It may even be assumed that just as the unconsciousness affects us, so the increase in our consciousness affects the unconscious.

— C.G. Jung, *Memories, Dreams, Reflections*

On April 26, 2014, Poly Prep, at its 2014 alumni reunion day, dedicated a friendship bench to Poly's victims of sexual abuse.

A respectable crowd drawn from all segments of the Poly community gathered under a tent in the area outside and across from Poly Prep's library. A large podium, adorned with Poly Prep's ornate seal, stood to greet the only two speakers: David Harman, Poly Prep's headmaster since 2000, and David Hiltbrand, Class of 1971, a survivor of Foglietta's sexual abuse and the man who, in 1991, reported his childhood abuse to William M. Williams, Poly's then headmaster.

Here are the words of the two Davids:

Headmaster David Harman:

Good afternoon. Thank you all for being here for this important event. We have wonderful representation from trustees, faculty, staff, administration, alumni, and, most importantly, from survivors.

Jim [Zimmerman '82] and David [Hiltbrand '71] welcome back.

This is a very important moment for all of us. I want to begin by again apologizing for the school. Scott Smith, the chairman of the Poly Prep trustees and present Poly parent, and I sent a written apology several months ago, but I now want to say again in person how profoundly sorry I am for the pain and suffering you (David and Jim) and the other survivors endured and continue to endure.

Thank you for your courage and your conviction. Poly failed to protect you. Your legacy is that you have our pledge, our solemn oath, never to let this kind of abuse happen again at this school.

We gather today to dedicate this bench and this space. I wrote the following to the faculty and to the trustees earlier this week: The purpose of the bench, which will have an inscription on the front, is to remember the pain and suffering of the survivors, known and unknown, to promote further healing and reconciliation, and to be a symbol of Poly Prep now being a safe place where we are doing everything possible to protect the children in our care.

The inscription on the front of the bench reads: "Dedicated to members of the Poly community who suffered abuse while in our midst. We remember and affirm: No Poly student shall ever sit alone again. April 26, 2014."

David Hiltbrand will now speak.

David Hiltbrand:

I'd like to thank the headmaster for his generous remarks and for allowing me to be part of this ceremony.

I would imagine some of you are wondering, because I certainly have, why I am up here talking about things that occurred when I first started as a student at Poly nearly fifty years ago. I've been asked on occasion, "Why don't you just let it go?"

Here's why: when a boy is physically violated and sexually abused, a part of him, often a significant part of him, dies. Imagine if you will little thirteen and fourteen-year-old stroke victims dragging themselves around the corridors of the school. That's what you had for the twenty-five years that Philip Foglietta used his employment at Poly to prey on its students.

For the young victim, the immediate reaction is a profound sense of disassociation. You separate, split off from yourself. You will never again in this world feel entirely comfortable in your own skin. Then come the waves of confusion, shame, isolation, fear, and overwhelming sadness. The chronic nightmares never slacken. As these children mature, alcoholism and drug addiction become endemic. Among men, this toxic knot inside them usually manifests itself as depression and rage. The worst stigma is that you will never be able to love another human being, or receive their love.

Who would not do everything in his power to jettison this insufferable burden? At whatever the cost. So the fact that almost all victims of child sexual abuse carry these wounds still raw and gaping to their deathbeds underscores just how persistent that pain is.

By the way, I use the terms victim and survivor interchangeably. Don't read anything into that.

I should also say that I am not a representative of or spokesman for the other survivors. A few support my being here, others condone it, and some are fiercely opposed to my participation today.

That is to be expected. The rift between the school and the survivors has been deep. Over the years, the survivors have felt abandoned, betrayed and revictimized; lied to and lied about. I imagine the school has felt its good reputation was being tarred by the actions of one monster. That the victims perhaps harbored an unspoken agenda to damage the school, seeking vengeance more than vindication. And I'm sure there was a concern that offering any sort of compensation would result in a flood of copycat claims.

And so we stand here today. This is the first time I have set foot on the Poly grounds since the day I graduated in 1971. I've found myself flooded with long-forgotten memories. Some of them creepy, but a number of them positive.

That's the danger when we put up walls—as I did to my schooldays. We end up closing ourselves off to more than we intended, more than we can afford. I might never have returned here, but I felt it was important to acknowledge the measures Poly has taken this year—the apology and the installation of this bench. These are the first real steps towards reconciliation in this long, bitter dispute, and I commend the school and the current administration for taking them. I believe that even our worst transgressions cannot do us permanent harm if we acknowledge them, express genuine remorse, and do everything in our power to atone for them. I am encouraged to think that Poly is on that path.

How are Poly's recent efforts being received by the survivors for whom this bench is in part intended? I can tell you that for a few of us, this is a singularly meaningful and moving day. Others will presumably come over with time if Poly's spirit remains open. But there are many whose souls were so incinerated by what happened to them here as children that they are never coming back in any sense. Those are the victims who need our thoughts and our prayers. So in conclusion I ask those of you who wish to, to join me in a moment of silence for Poly's lost boys.

Thank you.[53]

After David's moving speech, I saw a number of men and women wipe tears from their eyes. Two of David's adult children, a son and a daughter, embraced their father. As did his ex-wife, who traveled to Poly Prep to add her support to her family.

One line in David's speech stood out to me: "The worst stigma [of childhood sexual abuse] is that you will never be able to love another human being, or receive their love."

At the time, I didn't understand those words and thought them to be an example of hyperbole, albeit sincere hyperbole. But, upon reflection, I was wrong. Dead wrong.

To not be able to love another human being or receive the love of another human being. What an awful plight. What could be worse?

Love is light. Love is the manifestation of God on earth. A world without love, where one cannot give or receive love to anyone else, is a world of complete darkness ... cold, bleak, heartless, scary. A world where pain and torment predominate and joy is nothing but an intangible concept far beyond one's clear conception, let alone grasp.

David Hiltbrand is not the only person who felt the absence of love or the mere hope of giving or receiving love after an assault on his childhood innocence. This condition is, tragically, all too common.

In *The 13th Boy: A Memoir of Education and Abuse*,[54] Stephen Fife, who attended the elite Horace Mann School in the Bronx in the late 1960s and early 1970s, describes how a charismatic English teacher used Stephen's natural teenage yearning to be considered "special" to inflict life-long wounds: physical, emotional, and spiritual. This teacher, well aware of the adolescent quest for love, a quest most acute during that awkward transitional phase from boyhood to manhood, stepped into the breach to provide a fraudulent, evil alternative to the ubiquitous teenage fear of the empty and the mundane.

The teacher, by force of personality and the adroit manipulation of a developing psyche, compelled the student, a mere boy, to sacrifice his body to the teacher to satisfy the teacher's twisted sexual longings. And, despite the woefully imbalanced power dynamic between the two, the boy still had the courage to resist, to not submit completely to the abuser's desires.

One's skin crawls after reading this book because Stephen Fife shows just how easy it is for a savvy adult to manipulate a child in such a despicable, life-altering, soul-shattering manner. Fife, however, was no shrinking violet, and—unlike many childhood sex abuse victims—at a young age, was able to appreciate the repugnancy of the abuse, the evil in the heart of the abuser, and the enormous damage it inflicted upon him.

As a mere eighteen-year-old, Fife confronted his abuser at his Manhattan apartment, stood face-to-face with his one-time mentor, and said, "You're a terrible, destructive person."

The abuser laughed in the face of Stephen Fife, a wounded and emotionally vulnerable young man, and told Fife that he was going to suffer a "terrible fate."

"You will join a long list of willful children who lashed out and couldn't make it on their own, what a shame to waste all that potential." [55]

Stephen Fife's description of what happened next should curdle the blood of every thinking and feeling man or woman:

"Suddenly [the abuser] was rattling off a list of twelve names with sardonic glee. Yes, this man of lists was giving me one more, the list of all the young men he'd driven to suicide. None of the names was familiar to me, but somehow that made what he said even more frightening." [56]

The abuser left Fife with a dire prediction:

"You will be the thirteenth boy, and you will have only yourself to blame. So don't come crying back to me." [57]

Stephen Fife wrote that after his Horace Mann ordeal he wanted to kill himself so badly that it was the subject of all his fantasies. [58]

"I had an almost sensual attraction to the idea of death, it was like an appetite, a hunger, that had to be fed." [59]

But Stephen Fife resisted the urge to take his own life. He refused to give his abuser the satisfaction of seeing his sick prophesy come to pass.

One of Fife's classmates, a promising boy who—like him—had rejected the abuser's more pernicious advances, was not so lucky. In his early twenties, this boy hanged himself in his parents' basement.[60] He, not Stephen Fife, was "the 13th boy" driven to suicide by one destructive man.

In the Poly Prep case, we pinpointed another half dozen young men—likely victims of Foglietta—who had committed suicide. Several had overdosed on drugs, a few had hanged themselves, and one of them, who had been an extremely popular manager of the football team, jumped into the path of a moving train.

These were some of the mortally wounded "lost boys" whom David Hiltbrand had referenced in his speech at Poly Prep. They too, like David, must have felt that they were incapable of giving or receiving love. But unlike David, they were unable to lift themselves out of the black hole of despair. Their childhood torments, which they were not able to overcome, made them view the world as a place without love. And without even hope for love.

The suicides of childhood sexual abuse victims is no doubt widespread. In the Poly Prep and Horace Mann examples, we have two abusers and at least nineteen boys or young men dead at their own hands. The number of suicides of sex abuse victims is not easily quantified, especially given victims' tendencies to take the facts about their sexual assaults to their graves and the awful stigma attached to suicide. But one does not need to be a genius or statistician to realize that this problem is endemic. There are no doubt thousands of lives snuffed out before their time because they fell victim to sexual predators.

But who is to blame for these deaths? The sexual abusers themselves, of course, bear primary responsibility. But they are not the only transgressors here. In the school context, the enablers, the facilitators of abuse, the administrators or fellow teachers who knew that a teacher or coach was abusing children but turned a blind eye or deaf ear to the plight of these children (and scores of others who followed in their footsteps), must bear *some* accountability.

Who speaks for those in the ground before their time? Who gives voice to the most abjectly voiceless, not just the dead, but the self-inflicted dead? Those dead who leave behind for those who loved them a long and diverse trail of pain, guilt, heartache, and self-recrimination.

What does the law, the sanctified, sanctimonious law, say to those many young men and women, or boys and girls, who killed themselves after suffering assaults on their bodies and spirits? And what does it say to those still living but engulfed by darkness, who fantasize about or long for death, who whisper to themselves, every day, the awful question: is today the day I will take my own life?

In New York State, at least, the law is exemplified through the recent decisions of the Honorable John G. Koeltl (of the Southern District of New York District Court) and the Honorable Denny Chin, the Honorable Reena Raggi, and the Honorable Guido Calabresi (all of the Second Circuit Court of Appeals) in the *Twersky v. Yeshiva University* case.

In that case, these experienced, brilliant, and highly esteemed judges, for reasons known only to them, have created a legal mechanism that allows a school and its administrators to escape *all* legal accountability for a prolonged and successful cover-up of sexual abuse.

The net result of the *Twersky* case is that if a school, like Yeshiva University, conducts a sex abuse cover-up long enough and well enough—guaranteeing that scores of children will be sexually assaulted *after* the school and its administrators know that certain employees have a propensity to sexually abuse children and have, in fact, abused numerous children on campus— it will face *zero* accountability.

These courts have arrived at this no culpability for heinous sex abuse cover-up result by constructing a grotesque fiction: that the abused children would have learned of the school's own misconduct (not just the misconduct of the abuser) had they merely conducted reasonable inquiries prior to their twenty-first birthdays.

This legal fiction in *Twersky* piggy-backed on the equally wretched 2006 New York Court of Appeals decision, *Zumpano v. Quinn*,[61] in which New York State's highest court held that forty-two men who claimed that as boys they had been sexually abused by Brooklyn priests were time-barred from bringing claims against the Archdiocese of Brooklyn because the plaintiffs would have ascertained the relevant facts had they made timely and reasonable inquiries after they were abused. The *Zumpano* Court ignored that the plaintiffs plausibly alleged that the Archdiocese of Brooklyn had engaged in a prolonged cover-up of the sexual abuse of children by its priests and did not provide the "relevant facts" to scores of children who made timely inquiries or sexual abuse complaints to its officials. (The author of the *Zumpano* opinion, the Honorable Carmen Beauchamp Ciparick—the first Hispanic and second woman to sit on the New York Court of Appeals, was hired as Of Counsel to Greenberg Traurig, LLP in 2012, when she reached the mandatory retirement age for New York State judges. Greenberg Traurig, LLP, as discussed previously, represented Yeshiva University in the *Twersky* case).

To Judge Koeltl and the Second Circuit panel, it did not matter that their ultimate finding of fact was so far-fetched that Yeshiva University's own attorneys made the deliberate, conscious choice to not even make the argument that now stands, in all its shame and absurdity, as the law of the land.

Yeshiva University's lawyers failed to argue, allude to, or even suggest that plaintiffs could have possibly discovered Yeshiva University's own misconduct at any time prior to December 2012. Yeshiva University's lawyers were so far off the beam that they categorically rejected the Title IX accrual standard—a plaintiff's actual or constructive knowledge of a school's deliberate indifference to sex abuse—which is the legal pedestal upon which the Second Circuit mounted its preposterous case-ending finding of fact.

Yeshiva University's attorneys knew that the school's own internal investigation, spearheaded by Sullivan & Cromwell, a leading New York City white shoe law firm, concluded, or at least suggested, that university administrators lied to and turned a blind eye and deaf ear to numerous students who were somehow able to summon the courage to report their abuse to school administrators.

The abusers were left in place in positions of power to abuse more innocent students. The complainants were told to move on and often warned that if they continued to press their accusations, they would do so at their own peril. Move on, boys. Move on.

The Second Circuit panel judges must thus have been holding their noses with one hand and crossing their fingers with the other when they ruled that the plaintiffs not only could have, but would have, discovered Yeshiva University's own knowledge and complicity had they promptly conducted a diligent inquiry or investigation after their sexual assaults. This was a patently absurd conclusion, as Yeshiva University's own internal investigation of sex abuse at YUHS demonstrated that complaining victims were stonewalled and deceived at every turn. Intimidation, deception, lies built upon lies, and cover-up, *not* disclosure and truth, were the order of the day at Yeshiva University.

So again I ask the question: what does the law, in 2016, say to those who, after being raped in body and mind, could no longer see the light—or the mere possibility of love—and surrendered to the darkness?

It says this: "Stay down in the muck! Roll over in your dusty graves, leave us the hell alone, and let these schools continue to bask in their faux glory and prestige, shaping the impressionable minds of our children. And get this through your skulls: no one hears you; no one wants to hear you; no one even wants to think of you anymore. Be gone! Be silent! Be forgotten!"

But what if another school, another set of administrators, learns that it has a sexual predator in its midst and decides, like so many schools before it, like Poly Prep, like Horace Mann, like Yeshiva University, like

Penn State, to initiate another cover-up, to let the abuser stay at the school, free to roam the hallowed halls or grimy locker rooms and pick his prey at will?

What does the law say to the students who attend or will attend that school?

"Good luck, boyo! Roll over and make room for the next poor soul who is designated to be the detritus, the collateral damage, of the status quo. And, yes, that poor soul may be you! But don't bother us with your nonsense. We have minds to mold, justice to dispense, and reputations to protect. So roll over and shut the hell up!"

The extant law on school cover-ups of sexual abuse in New York State is profane, vulgar, crude, disgusting, not fit for civil discourse. Cloaked in matter-of-fact language and half-assed legal precepts, the extant law on sex abuse cover-ups remains nothing short of an obscenity. The irrational and offensive law requires more than a civil and gentlemanly dissection. (I've tried that course, again and again, without much success). It requires action, not just words, and a conscious commitment—by judges and legislators—to fix that which is clearly broken.

The repulsive yet prevailing judicial mindset I describe, this exemplification of the law of the land, is real, not imagined. But it is not acceptable. The execrable status quo—a get-out-of-jail-free card for schools and administrators who successfully cover-up the sexual abuse of their students—is simply not acceptable.

How can men and women of good will respond to such a frontal assault on our notion of right and wrong? And, more importantly, how can we persuade those who were sexually abused and forsaken by those entrusted to care for them that life is worth living, that the pain will recede, that light will eventually break through the darkness, and that love is always stronger than hate? [62]

For starters, we can say this: "I, for one, with my myriad faults and deficiencies, will stand up for you. I will speak for you. I will fight for you. I will try my best to lead you from the darkness to the light. To show you that love is always possible. No matter what has happened to you. No matter who has abused you. No matter who has forsaken you.

"You need to keep in mind several fundamental truths: Love is never dead; love is immortal; love is the way, the journey, to the light. Nothing will ever change that. It is the secret of life. You need to discover that secret sooner rather than later. For if you do, it will set you free. It will inspire you in life and, when it is your time (and not a minute before then), it will even comfort you, caress you, hug you, in death."

The lost boys and lost girls, no matter where or on what plane they reside or exist, may still be found. Nothing or no one is, or needs to be, lost forever.

But we need to look for them before we can find them. And, at the threshold, as painful as it may be, we need to think about them and their horrific experiences. For if we fail to do so, if we choose to kick *their* painful and ugly memories into the dark corners of *our* consciences, we condemn these lost boys and girls to the abyss.

And what will that say about us?

CHAPTER THIRTY-FOUR

The Cave

If there is to be reconciliation, first there must be truth.

— Timothy B. Tyson, *Blood Done Sign My Name: A True Story*

On the morning of April 26, 2014, I drove into the Lower East Side of Manhattan and picked up my Poly Prep classmate, Jim Zimmerman, in front of his office building on East 10th Street, just off Avenue L. Jim works for the New York City Department of Education. He attempts to help troubled, at-risk, and academically challenged youths obtain good jobs.

The evolution of my relationship with Jim Zimmerman was one of the side benefits of my legal services in the Poly Prep litigation. Thirty-two years after we graduated, we were no longer mere acquaintances; we were close friends. Jim has several rare combinations of positive attributes: toughness and compassion, integrity and empathy, intelligence and a keen sense of humor. He is a man with whom I would share a foxhole (or, more practically, a meal) any time, any place.

Now, less than a year-and-a-half after the Poly Prep settlement, I was on my way to my alma mater, with Jim, for the long anticipated reconciliation ceremony.

Before I picked up Jim that morning, while I was driving south on the Palisades Parkway, I received a call from J. Paggioli.

"Still going to the dog and pony show?" he asked.

"Yup," I replied.

"They're using you, Kev. I'm telling you. This is total bullshit. It's all public relations. And I'm right about this. I'm not a Jap in a cave."

J. was referring to a conversation earlier in the week when I had told him that he reminded me of a Japanese soldier emerging from a cave on an island somewhere deep in the Pacific, years after World War II had ended, still thinking that the war was ongoing and active.

I dismissed J. curtly and hung up. I believed that my metaphor was accurate and that it was imperative for J. and all the other plaintiffs to move past the hate and the rage and accept the embrace of the Poly Prep community, belated as it may have been.

I also knew that J. would never do that. He was destined to stew in the juices, the venom, of his anger over the destruction of his childhood innocence. Fueled by rage, not just by his childhood abuse but by how shabbily Poly Prep treated him when he came forward to tell his horrific tale and demand some measure of justice, J. will never make peace with Poly Prep.

After the speeches of the two Davids, I milled about Poly Prep, mostly in the grassy knoll area opposite the front entrance. I talked to Arnie Mascali and Gary Hanna, both members of the Class of 1984 and starting infielders on our 1982 Varsity Baseball squad. They were both warm and engaging and extremely cordial and pleasant. We joked that our high school batting averages went up ten points or so every year.

I also talked to Michael Kalmus, an attorney, and another Poly Prep alumnus, Class of 1971. Mike had represented Poly Prep in the final settlement negotiations with my clients, and he and I, with much in common, had become friends. I even requested and obtained his assistance in the *Twersky v. Yeshiva University* sex abuse case which we filed in the U.S. District Court for the Southern District of New York in July, 2013.

I left Poly Prep, however, soon after I saw Ronald Dugan,[tt] clad in a navy sports jacket, light blue shirt, dark gray pants, and straw hat, laughing and yucking it up with a few alumni. Dugan, the long-time Varsity Wrestling coach at Poly, had been Headmaster William M. Williams's right-hand man for many years. When I had deposed him months earlier, he had been so evasive and patently deceptive that I wondered if he would say "I don't recall" if I asked him to state his name at the end of the deposition. His mere presence at this "reconciliation" event reminded me of Poly Prep's prolonged obstruction and deceit in the *Zimmerman* litigation and offended my sensibilities.

As I drove back to Rockland County in the early afternoon, I thought about all the pictures of Poly Prep's athletic teams, located in the basement of the school, which I had looked at before the bench dedication ceremony. Poly Prep had retouched the team photographs for football and baseball for Coach Foglietta's entire tenure (1966 to 1991), and had removed each and every image of Foglietta. This was a professional job. There were no black or white patches, or outlines or shadows, where Foglietta had stood. If one did not know any better when looking at these photographs, one would think that Foglietta had never been there.

But that was a carefully created myth, a creature of public relations, rather than the cold, hard truth. Phil Foglietta had been there. And for a quarter of a century. The boys he had raped and abused, whose lives he had damaged, often grievously, sometimes irreparably, including two friends from the class right behind me who failed to make thirty, seemed to stare at me from these photographs.

But what, if anything, did they want to tell me?

The next Monday morning, when I returned to work, I sent an email to David Harman and several other Poly Prep administrators, thanked

---

[tt] This is a pseudonym.

them for inviting me to the bench ceremony, and applauded their sincere attempt to foster reconciliation between the school and Foglietta's victims.

I did not receive the courtesy of any replies to my email.

In July 2015, more than a year after the bench ceremony, I received an email from Dr. John S. Smolowe, Poly Prep Class of 1964. Dr. Smolowe, a Yale-educated psychiatrist with a long and distinguished medical career, now resides in Menlo Park, California. He told me that he had attended the April 26, 2014 bench ceremony at Poly Prep, as part of his class's fiftieth year reunion celebration, and wanted to provide me with some relevant information.

According to Dr. Smolowe, he was present for the bench dedication ceremony, and heard David Harman emphasize the school's purported desire to reconcile with the victims of sexual abuse, help them through the healing process, and bring them back into the Poly Prep community.

Later that same day, within a few hours of the bench ceremony, David Harman divided the Class of 1964 reunion attendees into two groups and together with Robert Aberlin, Poly Prep's Director of Finance, lectured each group, in turn, about the advances Poly Prep had made in addressing complaints of abuse.

During the Poly Prep litigation, I had come to know and like Robert Aberlin. He is extremely intelligent, funny, and charming. At one of our first meetings, he gave me a tape of a documentary he had directed and produced which showed how the Poly Prep community had banded together and honored the seven "Poly boys" who had been killed at the World Trade Center on 9/11. In the video, when Lisa Della Pietra, who was five years behind me at Poly, spoke about losing her beloved brother, Joseph, on that horrific day, I could tell by looking into her soulful eyes how much she loved and missed her brother and surmised, correctly as it turned out, that this was a rare, beautiful, and special person.[63]

Robert Aberlin has large, bright, puppy-dog eyes, with deep, dark circles underneath. I watched him, at various times, when he listened to my clients' stories about their childhood experiences and the myriad pathologies that flowed from them. He would tilt his head and his extraordinarily expressive eyes would well up; he often looked like he was about to cry. He projected a vast reservoir of empathy and understanding.

At the Class of 1964 reunion, one of Dr. Smolowe's classmates asked David Harman if they could discuss their dissatisfaction with how Poly Prep had previously handled complaints of abuse.

According to Dr. Smolowe, Harman responded that the current administration had no involvement in handling complaints of abuse as all abuse had occurred well before any members of the current administration had arrived. The latter part of that statement was patently false, as Steve Andersen, Poly's then Director of Operations, was Foglietta's assistant coach on the Varsity Football team from about 1977 until Foglietta's forced retirement in 1991.

Robert Aberlin, who was standing right next to Harman, then told Dr. Smolowe's group of about twenty persons: "You have to understand that they were threatening to burn the school down."

Aberlin made clear that the "they" he was talking about were the plaintiffs in the *Zimmerman v. Poly Prep* litigation. David Harman stood right next to Aberlin, silent, and thus at least tacitly endorsed Aberlin's statement.

At that point, Dr. Smolowe raised his hand and challenged Aberlin's assertion about these sex abuse victims. He said, "please do not continue to demonize the victims. It's in very bad taste, and I would guess that it's likely prohibited by the settlement you reached."

Even then, neither Aberlin nor Harman apologized for the statement about the *Zimmerman* plaintiffs threatening to burn the school down, retracted the statement, or tempered the statement in any way. Dr. Smolowe worried that he may have spoken too forcefully, but a group of classmates and their wives came up to him later and thanked him for voicing what they too had been feeling.

David Harman and Robert Aberlin, eager to cast Poly Prep, and themselves and their fellow administrators, in a good light on this day of "reconciliation," thought nothing of throwing my guys under the bus at the first, extraordinarily benign, sign of pressure. They neglected to inform the Class of 1964 reunion attendees that we had reached out to Poly Prep for such reconciliation long before a lawsuit was filed or, for that matter, was even on the horizon. That irrefutable fact would have ruined the day's narrative.

"They were threatening to burn the school down."

Many Poly Prep alumni, faculty, and board members attended the bench dedication ceremony with pure and noble intentions. I'm sure that some of these people share my outrage that several Poly administrators took it upon themselves to disparage the *Zimmerman* plaintiffs, while two of these plaintiffs were enjoying Poly's beer, soda, and burgers less than the length of a football field away from the scene of the offending utterance.

Reconciliation is *still* a worthy goal. But it takes two to tango. And it needs to start with an honest dialogue about how on one bright, sunny day Poly Prep administrators publicly claimed to initiate meaningful reconciliation with sex abuse survivors while, on that same day, made or endorsed a statement that falsely depicted the *Zimmerman* plaintiffs as irrational, dangerous, out-of-control, flamethrowers.

Poly Prep owes my clients, my friends, yet another apology. And Poly needs to mean it this time. Action is now required. Hollow words will no longer suffice.

Part Four:

A Son Rises

When a relationship of love is disrupted, the relationship does not cease. The love continues; therefore, the relationship continues. The work of grief is to reconcile and redeem life to a different love relationship.

—W. Scott Lineberry, *Tragedy and Loss and the Search for Jesus*

CHAPTER THIRTY-FIVE

Thunder and Lightning

The timeless in you is aware of life's timelessness. And knows that yesterday is but today's memory and tomorrow is today's dream.

— Kahlil Gibran, *The Prophet*

On October 25, 1996, I was waiting to meet a young woman of Ecuadorian descent, Roxanne Viteri, at a Spanish restaurant in Midtown Manhattan. Roxanne was more than a half hour late to our blind date, and I would have left prior to her arrival if she had not been my mother's friend and co-worker (they were both kindergarten teachers at a public school in Sunset Park, Brooklyn).

But, soon after Roxanne entered the restaurant, a bit frantic and wild-eyed, I was glad that I stayed. Roxanne was attractive, with beautiful brown hair, piercing brown eyes, and smooth, light-bronze skin. She was also intelligent, curious, and funny. Roxanne even laughed at most of my jokes. I took it as a good omen when on the very next evening after we first met, the New York Yankees clinched the 1996 World Series against the Atlanta Braves.

After a short—at least for half an Irishman—five-and-a-half year courtship, we were married on April 27, 2002 at St. John the Baptist Church in Piermont, New York. Almost four years later, in January 2006, we were thrilled when Roxanne's doctor told us that she was pregnant. Roxanne is a nurturing and kind woman. I had no doubt that she would make an excellent mother.

On Saturday night, October 27, 2006, Roxanne and I drove to a new Italian restaurant on North Middletown Road in Nanuet. Roxanne was now more than eight months pregnant. We were met at the restaurant by Peter and Maria Dene, our close friends from Pearl River.

Peter, about ten years older than I (then in his early fifties), had grown up in Sunset Park, Brooklyn, in a two-family home on 58th Street between 9th Avenue and Fort Hamilton Parkway. My father— who was about fourteen years older than Peter—and his parents lived in an apartment building right across the street. When Peter was about ten or eleven, my dad would occasionally throw a baseball with him in the street between each of their homes. My father even took young Peter to Yankee Stadium a few times to watch the Yankees and the great Mickey Mantle, the boyhood hero of both.

When my parents were married in January 1963, they moved into the second floor apartment in Peter Dene's parents' house. They lived in that 58th Street apartment when Dennis, I, and Sean were born, and did not move out until the Summer of 1969—during the latter part of my mother's pregnancy with Deirdre—when my parents bought their house on Kimball Street. According to Peter, his twin sisters, Lisa and Linda, treated Dennis and me like human dolls, frequently changing us into the outfits of their girlish whims. (I can neither confirm nor deny that account).

After my parents moved to Kimball Street in 1969, I did not see Peter Dene again until early 1995, when he and his lovely wife, Maria, walked into my office with a legal matter for me to handle. We soon became fast friends, as—among other things—Peter rooted for the Yankees with as much ardor (or more) than I. We had been to many games together, including, notably, Game Five of the 2001 World Series, when Scott Brosius homered in the bottom of the ninth off the Arizona Diamondbacks' closer, Byung-Hyun Kim, to tie the game, and Alfonso Soriano singled sharply to right to score Chuck Knoblauch with the winning run in the bottom of the twelfth, and Game Seven of the Yankees' 2003 American League Championship Series win over the Red Sox—when Aaron Boone punctuated the Yankees' epic comeback with a game-winning homer to left field off Red Sox knuckleballer, Tim Wakefield.

On this Saturday evening, Maria and Peter were giving Roxanne and I some parenting tips. They had two young adult children, Peter Vincent and Annmarie, who were the type of caring, loving people that we hoped our soon-to-be-born son would turn out to be. But I had not really started to focus too much on how fatherhood would change my life. Roxanne's due date was November 20th, so I figured I had some time—almost a month—to prepare myself for the upcoming sea change. Emotionally, mentally, I had not yet checked in.

I had turned forty-two exactly a week before (on October 20th). Roxanne had turned forty on October 17th. I was an emotionally immature and extremely self-centered man. My needs and my wants always came first. Roxanne was not blind to this dynamic. By October 2006, after being married to me for more than four years, she resented my me-first approach and had grown somewhat sullen and distant. I was not the man, the husband, she wanted me to be. I was not able to love with my whole heart. I protected that last layer, the innermost chamber, with steely resolve. And nothing was going to change that.

A few minutes after we ordered our meals, but before we were served, Roxanne's water broke. We rushed out to our car and drove home to get Roxanne's baby preparation bag. She called her doctor, took a shower, changed into fresh clothes, and we headed to Good Samaritan Hospital in Suffern, New York, which had recently completed a first-class renovation of its maternity wing.

Back at the restaurant, Peter and Maria explained to the owners that Roxanne was about to have a baby and that we had left the restaurant in due haste. The owners didn't give a damn and made Peter and Maria pay for our entrees. Not surprisingly, and fittingly, this restaurant didn't last too long and shuttered its doors a few months later.

When we arrived at Good Samaritan—at about 8:00 p.m.—a doctor examined Roxanne and determined that she had a long way to go, at least eight hours. Roxanne settled into her bed and after a few minutes we began to talk about the name of our son. For months our debate had been raging. I wanted to name our boy, "Dennis," in honor of my brother. Roxanne liked the name "Dennis" but she loved the name "Ryan." She wanted to name the baby "Ryan Dennis Mulhearn." I too liked the name "Ryan"—it was strong, Irish, and masculine—but I could not fathom tabbing our son, my son, with any first name other than "Dennis." A middle name was an insufficient honor to my brother.

The maternity nurse, a lovely young brunette named Jeanine, over-heard our conversation.

"You're thinking of naming your son, 'Ryan?'" she asked.

Roxanne nodded.

"My sister's boy's name is 'Ryan,'" she said. "He cries all the time, so everyone in my family calls him 'Cryin' Ryan.'"

When Jeanine left the room, I pounced.

"Roxanne, did you hear that? Can you imagine calling your child, 'Cryin' Ryan?' What an awful nickname. We can't do that to our son, can we?"

Roxanne, in extreme pain and discomfort, smiled wanly.

"OK, Kevin, you win. We'll call him 'Dennis.'"

I squeezed Roxanne's hand. She had not countered, as I would have, that "Dennis the Menace" was a far more commonly heard nickname—invoked in literature, film, and television—than "Cryin' Ryan."

I knew that Roxanne's assent to the name "Dennis" was a gift to me. I let Roxanne pick our boy's middle name. After much vacillation, she chose "Luke."

As we had rushed out of the Nanuet restaurant before any food was served, I was famished. After triple-checking with the doctor that there was no chance that our baby would be born in the next hour, I asked Roxanne if she would permit me to go to a nearby diner to pick up some food. She told me that she didn't mind, but to hurry back.

As I jumped into my car and headed to the diner (which was just five minutes away), I heard a thunder clap in the distance. On my way back, after I had picked up a couple of cheeseburgers, the heavens opened up and it started to pour. By the time I arrived back at the Good Samaritan parking lot, a thunderstorm was in full bloom: lightning sparked all around me and thunder, loud and frequent, rattled my ears.

It was raining too hard for me to leave my car, so I sat in the front seat, as the heavy raindrops battered my car's hood and windshield and, as lightning continued to flash and thunder continued to roar, I thought about the thunderstorm that occurred the night my brother Dennis died, a few hours after I broke the awful news to my father. This storm to-night was just as fierce, just as powerful. I smiled; this is bizzaro world staring me in the face. Every horrific event, every awful feeling, every destroyed dream that occurred on August 24, 1993 was about to be flipped. Pain was about to be transformed into joy; grief into gratitude; regret into hope. On this October night, the lightning and thunder were about to herald a celebration, not a requiem.

That night, October 27, 2006, I had planned to watch Game Five of the World Series between the Detroit Tigers and St. Louis Cardinals. As the rain continued to pelt my car, I realized that there was some kind of bizzaro symmetry at play in the world of baseball, as well. On the night of October 20, 1990, our twenty-sixth birthday, as Dennis was losing his sanity, his connection with reality, the Oakland A's, skippered by Tony LaRussa, were swept out of the World Series by the underdog Cincinnati Reds, the Nasty Boys and friends.

Tonight, October 27, 2006, was ninety-seven years to the date my grandfather, Poppy, was baptized and twenty-eight years to the date Poppy died. Dennis was twenty-eight when he drowned, just a stone's throw away from Camden Yards. Tonight the script would be reversed.

If I had access to a bookie, I would have bet everything I owned, every last nickel, that tonight the St. Louis Cardinals, managed by Tony La-Russa, would win the World Series. Tonight Tony LaRussa would not skulk his way into the dark night a beaten, defeated man. Tonight he would become a World Champion. Tonight was a night for birth, not death. Renewal and redemption were in the air. I realized that if I tried to explain any of this to anyone, he or she would have thought that I was as crazy as my brother had been. But that didn't matter to me. I knew in my heart, deep in my soul, that I was right. The universe would soon be correcting itself.

When the rain slowed to a drizzle, I left my car and returned to the hospital's maternity ward.

"What took you so, long?" Roxanne asked.

"Oh, nothing, it just rained like hell for a few minutes," I replied.

As I sat next to Roxanne and unwrapped a cheeseburger, I saw that there was a television in the back of the room. At that minute the Cardinals and Tigers were in the early innings of Game Five. I was tempted, so tempted, to slink back and turn on the game, but I could not do it. I could not abandon Roxanne as she was suffering, as she was about to give birth to our child, our son. Besides, I already knew who was going to win.

(On October 27, 2006, when Adam Wainwright fanned Brandon Inge on a nasty slider, the St. Louis Cardinals defeated the Detroit Tigers 4 to 2 to take the World Series four games to one).

On the morning of October 28, 2006, at about 6:45 a.m., Roxanne—with a look of fierce determination—pushed through the labor pains one last time. Our child pushed his way into the light and introduced himself to me and his mother. We had waited so long for this moment, feared it would never come, and imagined it a thousand times. But the anticipation, the imagination, the dreams, paled in comparison to the reality:

our living, breathing, bald, beautiful, brown-eyed, baby boy was in our arms.

I felt something else that morning. I felt the presence of my brother Dennis in the room. There were no tangible signs, no visions, no voices, no flickering lights, no electric sparks, but I knew he was there anyway. I knew it just as surely as I knew my own name. As soon as my son was born, I was engulfed by a feeling, a wave, of tranquility, contentment, happiness. The feeling was beyond description. I had goosebumps up and down both arms, and my fingers and toes tingled; all my sensations were heightened. I felt the blessing of my brother Dennis for his namesake. I felt, from my head to my toes, my brother's love. For my child . . . and for me. I felt, for the first time in my life, pure, unadulterated joy.

After a few minutes, the nurse took Dennis from me and placed him in a crib-like basket. I placed my fingers on Dennis's right hand. His fingers curled around my thumb. Jeez, that's a pretty big hand for a baby, I thought. Maybe he'll be able to throw a split-finger fastball. I couldn't help myself, even at that precious moment, from thinking about baseball.

I left the hospital room to retrieve Roxanne's mother, Maria, from the waiting room to introduce her to her first grandchild. As I walked the halls in the hospital, I realized that I felt discernibly freer and lighter. I had not realized how heavy my chain of grief—which I had carried for thirteen years—had been until the links melted off my back the moment my son was born.

The world was still far from perfect. But I had been blessed with a rare gift: the ability to love with my whole heart. The ability to be a father to a son. I was, once again, that lucky kid. The universe had opened itself up to me—for just a split second—and revealed its wonders, its potential. It had shown me the very best that it had to offer.

I vowed to myself that I would not be fool enough to waste this chance.

CHAPTER THIRTY-SIX

Redemption

Baseball is a game dominated by vital ghosts; it's a fraternity, like no other we have of the active and the no longer so, the living and the dead.

— Richard Gilman

On November 4, 2009 Mariano Rivera once again jogged to the mound at Yankee Stadium (albeit one across the street from the old ballpark), to the inspiring sounds of Metallica, needing just five more outs to clinch a World Series for the Yankees. He was pushing forty now, much closer to the end than to the beginning, but his team still relied on him more than any other player. He was the difference maker.

With nerves of steel and extraordinary mental toughness, he made tough pitch after tough pitch. He was not nearly as fast as he once was, and he was secretly nursing a rib-cage injury, but Mariano went about his business, impervious to the pressure, and did his job. When the last ball was hit meekly to the Yankees' second baseman and thrown to first for the final out, Mariano's mask of serious purpose fell off into a smile of unbridled joy. He did it once again. Incomparable, unforgettable, a man of class and integrity, a role model for us all.

The Yankees' 2009 World Series victory reminded me anew of the potential for each of us to find our better angels, to fulfill our promise, and to not let a momentary defeat—awful as it may be— prevent us from reaching for the stars. Thank you, Mariano. And folks, please, don't tell me it's just a game.

Baseball, while not a magic elixir which can numb our pain or strike at the heart of the omnipresent evil lurking in our midst, still matters to me. And it always will. For it helps me, like the sun peeking from a burst of clouds, to see the good, remember the innocent, and never forget that our limitations are only those which we impose upon ourselves.

CHAPTER THIRTY-SEVEN

The Bostonians, Redux

Love means to commit oneself without guarantee, to give oneself completely in the hope that our love will produce love in the loved person. Love is an act of faith, and whoever is of little faith is also of little love.

— Erich Fromm, *The Art of Loving*

More than a year after my father died (on August 27, 2010), his wife Willie called me on my cell and in a frantic voice beckoned me to visit her at her Nanuet apartment.

"I have something really important to tell you, and I need to talk to you in person," she said.

When I arrived at Willie's Normandy Village apartment, I took a seat on the sofa. To my left, empty, stood my father's brown Lay-Z-Boy chair, a Christmas gift from my siblings and me. A lump formed in my throat. My grief over my father's death was still sharp. His absence, the loss of his voice, especially in this room where we had spent hundreds of hours watching baseball and other sports, was profound.

"I miss your father, very much," said Willie. "So I went with my friend Donna to see a medium the other day."

I leaned forward on the sofa. "Did his spirit talk to you?" I asked.

"No," she shook her head. "But Dennis did. Dennis came through."

Willie told me that the medium said that a strong spirit of a young man was fighting to be heard, and that he even identified himself by name.

"Tell my brother that I didn't kill myself. It was an accident."

The medium told Willie that the spirit was showing him a large body of water.

"Yes, he drowned!" Willie exclaimed.

"It's important for him to know that it was an accident. I didn't want to kill myself. He needs to know that.

"And thank him for the shoes. I really appreciate the shoes."

Willie told me that the spirit talking to this medium went on and on about the shoes.

"He couldn't stop talking about the shoes, and I had no idea what the hell he was talking about."

Willie had asked each of my siblings if they knew anything about the meaning of the shoes. Sean, Deirdre, and Thomas all drew a blank.

After my meeting with Willie, I called Sean and tried to refresh his recollection about the shoes.

"Don't you remember that we couldn't find any shoes for him and I ended up giving you a new pair of Bostonians to take to the funeral director?"

"Honestly, Kevin," Sean replied, "I really don't remember anything about that at all."

When I hung up, I thought about this for a while. No one in the universe, other than me, could remember or verify that I had given Dennis my new pair of tassled wing-tips for his eternal rest. This was a secret known only to me and Dennis. And there was no way I could prove that this had happened but I still knew that it was true. This was the communication, albeit through several surrogates (Willie and the medium), that I had been looking to receive from my brother since August 24, 1993, the day he died.

I have refrained from learning any additional details about Willie's experience with the medium. I do not need to know her name. I do not need to know where her performance took place. I do not even need to know her reputation for veracity and accuracy. [64]

For me, the narrative as it stands is enough. The medium's translation of the spirit's message, intended to help me understand and come to peace with the cause, means, and motive of a death that occurred almost two decades earlier, is a great comfort, a salve, a blessing.

I want to believe. Or maybe I need to believe. Either way, it doesn't really matter. The bottom line is that I believe. I stand with Carl Jung. I believe that the dead can communicate with the living. I believe that my brother did not intentionally take his own life.

Towards the end of Willie's conversation with the medium, she told Willie that Dennis was happy and that he was laughing and playing with some friends in a field.

It must have been a baseball field. I cannot imagine anything else.

CHAPTER THIRTY-EIGHT

To Dust

[F]or the first time in my life I saw the truth as it is set into song by so many poets, proclaimed as the final wisdom by so many thinkers. The truth—that Love is the ultimate and highest goal to which man can aspire. Then I grasped the meaning of the greatest secret that human poetry and human thought and belief have to impart: The salvation of man is through love and in love.

— Viktor E. Frankl, *Man's Search for Meaning*

On Saturday, May 9, 2015, the Braves, Pearl River Little League AA Division, lost a hard fought game to the Blue Jays, 9-5. My eight-year-old son Dennis had a rough day at the plate. After twice striking out looking and grounding to first, he had an opportunity to redeem himself in the last inning, when he strode to the plate with two outs and runners on first and third. Dennis struck out on a pitch over his head. At least he went down swinging.

In the dugout after the game I performed my glamorous duties as manager and threw all the catcher's gear, helmets, and bats into our team's black canvas bag. I stole a look at Dennis. He was sitting glumly, bravely trying to fight back tears.

"Are you crying, Dennis?" one of his teammates asked.

"No," he replied as only an eight-year-old can reply. "My eyes are sweaty."

I filled out the pitchers' log book at the Hopper, the Pearl River Little League clubhouse, and bought Dennis a bag of Skittles and a bottle of water. His mood improved. Dennis's old bat, the one he had been using all season, had bent at the barrel and needed to be discarded. So I took him to Modell's on Route 59 and picked up a new 29' Easton bat with a black handle and blue barrel.

The next day is Mother's Day. Dennis is eager to try out his new bat. At about 11:30 a.m. I start pitching to him in our backyard.

"Keep your shoulder in. Keep your eyes on the ball. Wait for it. And attack the baseball."

When he starts stepping in the bucket, I instruct him to practice stepping towards the plate without a ball being thrown. He does the necessary tap dance and when I start pitching to him again he begins to spray line drives all over the yard, including a bunch over the rocks and into the poison ivy patch that is at the back of our property.

"Attaboy, Dennis," I cry out after a solid hit. "That's the way to hit a baseball!"

At 12:30 p.m. my mom comes over to our house. Even in her seventies, my mother is blessed with a youthful sense of innocence and child-like wonder. A singer (her melodious voice commanded our Church congregation's attention when she sang Sunday hymns), dancer, actress, artist, and, last but not least, teacher, my mother has always been a beacon of love and light in my life. She has also been a superb moral guidepost, showing me with her actions, not just her words, how to make difficult decisions. I have always been able to count on my mother's support, in anything I do, with just about absolute certainty.

We stop playing for a few hours as we take my mother and Roxanne to Cassie's, a local Italian restaurant, for an early Mother's Day dinner. Sean meets up with us at Cassie's with his son Blake and Blake's mom,

Kenya, a warm, beautiful, black-haired, Dominican woman with a captivating smile.

After a delicious meal, we head back to the house. This time Dennis wants to play ball with his Uncle Sean. I ask Sean to help Dennis with his pitching mechanics.

Sean, in 1984, had been an All-City pitcher in Brooklyn for Poly Prep. After opening the season with thirty-five scoreless innings, Sean finished his senior year with a 9-0 record, a .70 earned run average, and an extraordinarily painful right elbow (he probably was a prime candidate for Tommy John surgery). He had an excellent fastball, an even better curve, terrific poise, and a fierce competitive streak.

As a sophomore when Dennis and I were seniors, in 1982, Sean was our number two pitcher and was instrumental in securing our Ivy League title. He bailed us out in a late season game against The Trinity School by shutting them out for three or four innings while we mounted a desperate comeback.

On this Sunday in May 2015, Sean can no longer throw with his nice easy motion because early onset Parkinson's has robbed his right arm of mobility and accuracy. His throws now are rigid flips, like a one-armed bandit at a casino. Sean ignores this physical insult without complaint. And he knows pitching. Our father taught him how to pitch.

"Take your time, Dennis," Sean instructs. "And come to a complete stop. Turn your shoulder, flip your glove away from one side of your body to the other, and make sure you step towards home plate. Where you step is where the ball is going to go." Sean demonstrates the proper pitching motion to Dennis. My son nods obediently and tries to execute his pitches.

After a few minutes, we begin to see the results. Dennis throws straight overhand with good velocity for an eight-year-old. He throws one knee-high strike after another.

"Stee-rike!" Sean bellows. Dennis laughs.

"That's the way an ump should call a strike. When I used to umpire, they could hear me all across Marine Park."

He is not exaggerating.

Sean, Kenya, and Blake leave and Dennis takes a break. An hour or so later, Tio Alfredo, who had taken his mother out to a Portuguese steakhouse in Pearl River, is ready to play some ball with his nephew.

Dennis is out for another hour and a half of practice: hitting, catching, pitching, throwing, grounders, flyballs, baserunning. He relishes the idea of trying to throw his father or uncle out trying to steal second base. After he throws each of us out about ten times, we are wiped out. Finito. Dennis has played baseball for a total of about four hours on this warm and sunny day.

On Tuesday, May 12, 2015, the Braves play the Phillies for the second time in the season. In the first game the teams battled to a 4-4 tie. Dennis's friend and classmate, Michael Squillini, is the star player for the Phillies. His dad, James, is the manager.

One of our aces, Michael Barresi, stands ready on the mound. He sets down the Phillies quickly in the first and in the bottom of the frame the Braves erupts for four runs, capped off by a two-run homer by Ryan Albin. But the Phillies battle back and score four runs to tie us in the second inning.

It is 4-4 with one out and two on in the top of the third when Michael Barresi reaches his maximum pitch count. I bring Dennis in to pitch. The first batter hits a booming double to left to make it 6-4, Phillies. From there, Dennis goes to work and retires the side on a strikeout and weak grounder to first.

In the bottom of the third we tie the game. Dennis is pitching extremely well. With his new efficient motion, he is a strike-throwing machine. He strikes out four of the next six batters. But he gives up a run in the top of the fifth when he walks a kid with two outs and the runner steals second and scores after the catcher's throw to third base, on another steal attempt, sails into left field. 7-6, Phillies.

In the bottom of the fifth, our first two batters strike out quickly. Our leadoff hitter, Michael Barresi, draws a four pitch walk. Dennis strides to the plate.

After taking a few pitches out of the zone, he takes two good swings but fouls the ball straight back both times. Two balls, two strikes, two outs. The pitcher throws a high fastball on the outer half of the plate. Dennis takes a hard swing and whacks the ball on a line just to the left of the second baseman. The ball finds the gap between the right fielder and right-center fielder and rolls all the way to the outfield fence. Dennis is flying around the bases. When he hits third, the shortstop has the ball a little bit behind second base. I send my son home anyway. "Go, go, go!"

Dennis does not break stride as he digs for home. The catcher catches the shortstop's throw on the first base side of home plate and reaches to tag Dennis. But he is too late. Dennis slides hard into the plate and kicks up a cloud of dust. "Safe!" the kid umpire shouts. 8-7, Braves.

But the game is not over. Dennis takes the mound in the sixth with a slim one run lead and the Phillies' top of the order coming up. He is pumped up now. Strike one, strike two, strike three. And again. Two outs, no one on. He is still a strike-throwing machine. With a 2-2 count on the Phillies' number three batter, a burly lefty, Dennis unleashes his best fastball. The hitter laces it to left just inside third base. Two outs, tying run on second.

Dennis is now a bit flustered but he continues to battle. On a 2-2 count, the Phillies' clean-up hitter swings through a low fastball and the ballgame is over. Braves 8, Phillies 7. On the way back to our car, I tell Dennis that in all the years I played baseball I only hit one game-winning home run.

"So that means we're tied, Dad," he replies.

I laugh. "Yup, pal. We're tied."

Dennis cannot yet see what I see. He cannot fathom that his every throw, his every catch, his every hit, transports me to another place where I am just a boy, where baseball means everything to me, where it binds me tightly to my brothers and my father.

My father taught his sons how to be men by teaching us how to play baseball. A game where failure is inevitable but not permanent. And not to be feared. Where success is borne through maximum effort and maximum effort only. Where luck, dumb, stupid luck, plays a major role in the ending of things.

But here's the thing to remember: the inevitable unfairness of this world should be an incentive, rather than a deterrent, to fight like hell for cosmic justice whenever you can find even the slightest potential for it. The barest glimmer. The tiniest spark.

While it may seem counterintuitive to some, the above rule is a necessary adjunct to the Golden Rule: *Do unto others as you would have them do unto you.* Without the adjunct, the Golden Rule is for all practical purposes meaningless. Or at least toothless.

I was lucky enough to have been taught this invaluable truth, in turn, by my paternal grandfather, Poppy, and my brother Dennis, and my father. Without realizing that school was in session, I frequently received this lesson from each of them. Often on a patch of grass or dirt.

"Attaboy, Dennis. That's the way to hit a baseball.

"C'mon, Thomas, keep your eyes on the ball. And don't try to kill it.

"Attaboy, Sean. Throw like you mean it. Just like you're playing catch with the catcher.

"Good job, Kev, way to turn that double play."

My father's commanding voice is forever locked into my memory. So are his expressions: his pride—bright, sparkling, dancing blue eyes—when we do something well; his agitation—hand on hip, lips curled into a sneer—when we don't perform up to his high standards; and his rage—face purple, with a throbbing neck vein to match—when we commit the mortal sin of not trying our absolute best. All of these priceless memories descend, like gifts to the pharaoh, from a gold-tinged platform, through a narrow baseball prism.

It is impossible for me to explain to Dennis, or anyone else for that matter, how deeply this game is ingrained into my own subconscious. How much and how vividly it brings back to life my own dear departed. How tightly it binds my family.

Time no longer matters. It is no longer relevant. Age is meaningless. I am not north of fifty. I am seventeen, or twelve, or—heaven help me— eight. Just starting to play baseball, just graduating from the patch of dirt with the black iron fence to the real baseball fields of Marine Park. Learning how to run the bases, to go on ground balls and hold up on balls in the air, to hook slide into a base, to drive an outside fastball to right field.

To still be able to dream freely. To believe that all things are possible. To live in communion with all whom I love, whether or not they remain sentient, living beings, to be touched, to be seen, to be heard. *Poppy ... Dennis ... Dad.* They remain real to me. Capable of both giving and receiving love. More real, for some inexplicable reason, when they emerge, surrounded by a cloud of dust, from the scattered folds of my memory.

"Helluva game, Dennis. Helluva game."

His eyes lock with mine. I wonder if when he is fifty—and I have probably long returned to the earth—he will remember this look in my sweaty eyes at this very moment.

There is nothing quite like it. Whether embodied in flesh or apparition, in body or spirit, my eyes tell a rich and complex story. And it is a baseball story but not really a baseball story. My eyes alone tell this story. And it is a story with but one theme.

"Do you get it? Do you understand what I'm trying to say to you, Dennis?"

"I know you love me, Dad ... and I love you too."

Father to son. Son to father. Parent to child. Brother to brother. Blood to blood. And dust to dust.

Dust. Sprinkled from high above with but one purpose: to mold the past into the present and the future. Dust. Not dirt. Dust. Tiny particles of diamond magic that bring us a glimmer of hope and illuminate the stepping stones that will permit us to escape—if only for a few precious moments—the quicksand pull of the chaos and the pathos.

Dust.

To dust.

Appendix

HORACE MANN REPORT HIGHLIGHTS
NEED FOR S.O.L. REFORM

by Kevin Thomas Mulhearn

(This article was originally published by the New York Daily News, as an I-Team blog entry—with a brief introduction by Michael O'Keeffe—on June 2, 2015).

This week, the Honorable Leslie Crocker Snyder (ret.), founder of the Manhattan DA's Sex Crimes Prosecution Bureau and co-author of New York State's Rape Shield Law, issued her Report on sexual abuse that occurred at the elite Horace Mann School in the Bronx in the 70s, 80s, and 90s. The Report, titled "Making Schools Safe," commissioned by the Horace Mann Action Coalition, concludes that at Horace Mann at least sixty-four students were sexually abused by as many as twenty-two faculty and staff. Judge Snyder's Report describes the scope and extent of the parade of sexual abuse at Horace Mann and makes pointed recommendations for how independent schools can protect our children. For anyone with children in New York schools, especially private schools, this thoughtful and insightful Report, despite (or maybe because of) its repugnant subject matter, should be required reading.

The squalid abuse facts themselves are horrendous in their own right but the most disturbing component of the Report is the craven response of various school officials and trustees to sex abuse complaints made by abused students. The Report describes a prolonged, multi-decade Horace Mann cover-up, highlighted by the loss or destruction of voluminous sex abuse records and the deliberate indifference of a former headmaster who himself engaged in the sexual abuse of young boys. Like with the Catholic Church, Horace Mann officials confronted with direct allegations of sex abuse by soul-shattered victims were too often far more concerned with protecting the reputations of both institution and sex predator employees than the children entrusted to their care.

The Report also states that when Horace Mann's acts and omissions were finally publicly revealed in 2012 (after Amos Kamil's groundbreaking *New York Times Magazine* story), Horace Mann's insurers concluded that all of the victims' claims were "fully defensible due to New York's statute of limitations." The insurers' position reflects accurately the status quo in New York State. This is the harsh reality: New York state and federal courts have worked overtime to ensure that schools that actively cover up the sexual abuse of students by teachers, coaches, and administrators, thus guaranteeing that more unsuspecting and innocent children will be sexually assaulted, will face no legal accountability once the schools' own misconduct is exposed.

Statutes of limitation derive from a public policy to make persons secure in their reasonable expectation that the slate has been wiped clean of ancient obligations. But they are designed to foster, not hinder, litigants' search for the truth. Statutes of limitation are not designed to protect an institution which actively conceals its own misconduct from legal culpability, but that is exactly how they are being used by schools and their partners in crime, enabling courts.

New York state and federal courts have concluded time and time again that because the abuse victims knew the identity of their abuser, and that their abuser was employed by the school, the victims—traumatized, sexually assaulted children—would have discovered the school's own facilitation of their abuse had they conducted a diligent post-abuse inquiry. This case-ending conclusion has been reached even when survivors allege that they did report their abuse to school officials, but were met with lies, threats of reprisal, and challenges to their credibility. This exalted legal standard, which has been embraced by the courts of this state like a long-lost child, is a perversion of justice and an insult to logic, decency, and common sense.

The real reason why these courts adhere to such a draconian and counterintuitive legal standard, which transmogrifies "justice" into "injustice" with the stroke of a pen, is an unstated but paramount policy. The courts are worried that Pandora's box will open if these "old" sex abuse cases gain traction. They are worried that they will be faced with a flood of litigation against complicit schools; accordingly, they hold their collective noses and continue to embrace legal fiction mounted atop legal fantasy. Again and again.

After one reads Judge Snyder's Report on Horace Mann, or the pleadings in the Poly Prep or Yeshiva University High School for Boys cases, however, the milquetoast foundation of this obstructive judicial policy crumbles in the face of the sordid, almost hard-to-imagine, facts. Schools and school officials that engage in such reprehensible conduct—that let children get raped by known sexual predator employees—deserve no protection, no financial relief, regardless of when their concealed bad acts finally get exposed (i.e., regardless of how long they succeed in their sex abuse cover-ups). The simplest solution, as proposed by Judge Snyder, is the enactment into law of the Child Victims Act, the latest version of a bill proposed by Queens Assemblywoman Margaret Markey, which would substantially reform and broaden New York's statute of limitations for sex abuse cases.

Adult survivors of childhood sexual abuse are no longer victims. After all, it takes enormous strength and courage for them to confront their abusers and their abusers' enablers and demand some measure of accountability. But unless this bill (or a similar version) passes, courts are likely to continue to deny survivors legal redress and will thus continue to reward schools for conducting successful and prolonged sex abuse cover-ups. This status quo, while absurd, grossly unfair, and violent to all principles of equity, is for now deeply entrenched in New York law.

Time will tell whether "truth and justice" is a guiding principle or an empty slogan in New York State. In this arena, where nothing less than the safety and well-being of our children is at stake, there is no more room for pussy-footing. The time for statute of limitations reform is now.

Notes

Chapter 1

[1] This theory was developed at length by Ernest Becker in his critically acclaimed and bestselling book, *Denial of Death* (MacMillan Publishing Company, 1973).

Chapter 4

[2] Jaeger, Lauren. "Brooklyn Legend: Jim McElroy." *Baseball Player Magazine*, July 1, 2010.

Chapter 10

[3] *See Zimmerman v. Poly Prep, CDS*, 888 F. Supp.2d 317 (EDNY 2012).

Chapter 13

[4] Kinsella, W.P. "Promise or Betrayal?: Living in a Field of Broken Dreams." *Chicago Tribune*, March 5, 2006.
[5] Amos Kamil, with Sean Elder, recently published a captivating book—*Great is the Truth: Secrecy, Scandal, and the Quest for Justice at the Horace Mann School* (Farrar, Straus and Giroux, 2015)—which demonstrates how difficult it is for childhood sex abuse survivors to obtain justice in any meaningful sense.

Chapter 18

[6] Dennis John Mulhearn, with remarkable self-awareness, provided a vivid description and incisive analysis of his Messianic delusions in *Grand Delusions: A Story of Mental Illness, Hope and Love* (Hard Nock Press, 2015).

Chapter 23

[7] Jung, C.G. *Memories, Dream, Reflections* (Vintage Books, 1965) at 301.

[8] *Id.* at 312.

[9] *Id.*

[10] *Id.* at 312-13.

[11] Mulhearn, Dennis John. *Grand Delusions* (Hard Nock Press, 2015) at 176.

Part 3

[12] jackal. Dictionary.com. *Dictionary.com Unabridged.* Random House, Inc. http://dictionary.reference.com/browse/jackal

Chapter 28

[13] Hiltbrand, David. "Prestigious Poly Prep Grid Great's Abuse Drove Me to Drugs and Despair." *New York Post*, November 20, 2005.

[14] *Id.*

[15] *Id.*

[16] *Id.*

[17] *Id.*

[18] *Id.*

[19] Katz, Nancy. "Ex-Prep School Kid Files Sex Abuse Suit." *New York Daily News*, October 1, 2005.

[20] Hinch, Jim. "Dirt on Molest Coach." *New York Post*, November 17, 2005.

[21] *Id.*

[22] Cardwell, Diane. "Ex-Student Says Poly Prep Hid Years of Abuse by Coach." *New York Times*, November 17, 2005.

[23] *Id.*

[24] *Id.*

[25] 18 U.S.C. §§ 1962(c) & (d) (1988).

[26] 18 U.S.C. § 1341 (2000).

Chapter 29

[27] Jim Zimmerman and I both graduated from Poly Prep in 1982.

Chapter 30

[28] *McMunn v. Memorial Sloan-Kettering Cancer Center,* 191 F. Supp.2d 440, 445 (SDNY 2002).
[29] *Id.*
[30] Memorandum and Order of Hon. Cheryl L. Pollak, dated June 5, 2012 (Doc No. 265 of Case No. 09-CV-4586 at 20-73).
[31] *Zimmerman v. Poly Prep, CDS,* 888 F. Supp.2d 317 (EDNY 2012).
[32] *Id.* at 340.
[33] *Id.* at 340-41.
[34] *Id.* at 332-34. Judge Block dismissed the Civil RICO claims of the ten plaintiffs who did not make post-abuse contributions to Poly Prep.

Chapter 31

[35] Case No. 13-CV-04679
[36] Berger, Paul. "Student Claims of Abuse Not Reported by Yeshiva University." *The Jewish Daily Forward,* December 13, 2012.
[37] *See* Complaint, dated July 8, 2013 (Doc. No. 1 of Case No. 13-CV-04679).
[38] Transcript of August 6, 2013 Hearing before Hon. John G. Koeltl (SDNY), in *Twersky v. Yeshiva University,* Case No. 13-CV-04679, at 3-4.
[39] *Id.* at 4-6.
[40] *Id.* at 9.
[41] *Id.* at 13.
[42] *Id.* at 22.
[43] *Id.* at 23
[44] *Id.*
[45] The U.S. Supreme Court developed the standard for Title IX liability in a school sex abuse cover-up context in two cases: *Gebser v. Lago Vista Indep. School Dist.,* 524 U.S. 274 (1998) (which involved allegations that a teacher had sexually

abused a student), and *Davis v. Monroe County Bd. of Educ.*, 526 U.S. 629 (1999) (which involved allegations of a school's indifference to student-on-student abuse).

[46] See *Twersky v. Yeshiva University*, 993 F. Supp.2d 429 (SDNY 2014). Judge Koeltl emphasized that "plaintiffs' knowledge of their injuries started the clock," *Id.* at 441 n.2., and never stated or suggested that plaintiffs' Title IX injuries were their actual or constructive knowledge of Yeshiva University's deliberate indifference to sexual abuse at YUHS, rather than their sexual assaults. Judge Koeltl stated, to the contrary, that plaintiffs' deliberate indifference accrual argument "confused knowledge of a legal right with knowledge of injury[.]" *Id.* at 441 (citations omitted). He seemed to conclude, therefore, that the Title IX "injury"—at which time the three year statute of limitation began to run—was the time each plaintiff was sexually assaulted. In the appeal before the Second Circuit, Yeshiva University's attorneys—both in their brief and at oral argument—construed his decision to stand for that rule. If this, in fact, was his finding, Judge Koeltl was patently wrong on this point. The proper Title IX "injury" which triggers the applicable statute of limitations is a school's deliberate indifference to potential sex abuse which, in turn, caused a plaintiff to be harmed.

[47] See *Twersky v. Yeshiva University* (Case No. 14-365-CV), 579 Fed. Appx. 7, 9-10 (2d Cir. 2014).

[48] *Id.* at 9-10.

[49] *Id.*

[50] *Davis v. Monroe County Bd. of Educ.*, 526 U.S. 629, 645 (1999).

[51] See *id.* at 642-45.

[52] *Id.*

Chapter 33

[53] I obtained this transcript from a group email sent by a Poly Prep alumnus who attended the bench dedication ceremony and recorded the speeches of David Harman and David Hiltbrand.

[54] Fife, Stephen. *The 13th Boy: A Memoir of Education and Abuse* (Cune Press, 2015) at 149.

[55] *Id.* at 149.

[56] *Id.*

[57] *Id.*

[58] *Id.* at 155.

[59] *Id.*

[60] *Id.* at 158.

[61] *Zumpano v. Quinn,* 6 N.Y.3d 666 (2006). In this case, the Court of Appeals consolidated two cases from the Appellate Division. *Zumpano v. Quinn,* 12 A.D.3d 1096 (4th Dept. 2004), was an appeal of a Fourth Department decision. The case described in this book was *Estate of Boyle v. Smith,* 15 A.D.3d 338 (2d Dept. 2005). My friends, Michael Dowd and Paul Mones, two excellent lawyers and long-time advocates for childhood sexual abuse survivors, represented the forty-two plaintiffs in that case.

[62] The easiest and most practical way to change laws which protect schools and school administrators which succeed in covering up and/or facilitating the sexual abuse of students by school employees is to reform the archaic and manifestly unfair statutes of limitations for sex abuse survivors. In New York, Assemblywoman Margaret Markey has been trying to do so for almost a decade, with various proposed versions of a bill: "the Child Victims Act." The Appendix of this book is a slightly edited version of an article that I wrote for the *New York Daily News,* which advocates for statute of limitations reform and implores the New York State Legislature to pass the Child Victims Act. This article was originally published as a blog entry—with a brief introduction by Michael O'Keeffe—on June 2, 2015.

Chapter 34

[63] Lisa Della Pietra, the former Director of Alumni Relations at Poly Prep, is now embroiled in her own contentious litigation with Poly Prep.

Chapter 37

[64] I have read several books by renowned mediums: James Van Praagh (*Ghosts Among Us: Uncovering the Truth About the Other Side*) (HarperOne, 2009) and Mark Anthony (*Evidence of Eternity: Communicating with Spirits for Proof of the Afterlife*) (Llewellyn Worldwide, Ltd., 2015), and found their experiences, insights, and theories, fascinating and illuminating.

260 | KEVIN T. MULHEARN

Acknowledgments

First and foremost, I thank my family for its encouragement over the many years I was writing this book. Special thanks to my wife, Roxanne, son, Dennis, siblings, Sean, Deirdre, and Thomas, mother, Mary Ann, and her husband, Brian Lane, mother-in-law, Maria Viteri, brother-in-law, Alfredo Viteri, nephews, Michael Cid and Christian, dear friends and in-laws, Kenya Rodriguez, Jim Coombs, and Andrea Mulhearn, and step-mom, Willie, for their stalwart support. I'm blessed to have such a loving family.

I also extend my appreciation to my hard-working and loyal staff: Tom Butterworth, who worked diligently to convert the Word version of my manuscript into the finished book format, and made several excellent editorial suggestions; and Sally Riley, my lovely and cheerful secretary, who typed hundreds of draft chapters, always with a smile and never with a gripe.

This book changed dramatically in content and form over the last few years. I originally intended it to be a straight family narrative, but, as I became more and more embroiled in litigation on behalf of childhood sex abuse survivors, I eventually realized that such advocacy work had become an important part of my life and needed to be integrated into this book. I extend heartfelt appreciation and admiration to my many clients who as children experienced unimaginable nightmares—and as adults summoned the courage to demand some measure of accountability from those schools and school officials who facilitated the harm and pain inflicted upon them. These men and women—several of whom have become close friends—have taught me many valuable lessons. I wish them nothing but peace of mind and a steady and stable stream of love in their lives.

As to the baseball stories in this book, I freely admit that some of the details of the games I played in over thirty years ago, whether on the sandlot fields of Brooklyn, or for my high school and college teams, may not be one hundred percent accurate. These stories do represent, however, the best and most accurate reflection of my memory, flawed as it may be.

I extend thanks to Muhlenberg College's Sports Information Director, Mike Falk, for taking the time to search for the 1983 and 1984 scorebooks for the Muhlenberg College Mules Baseball team. Although Mike did not find any scorebooks, he did find the final statistics for both seasons, which enabled me to verify several facts about my less than scintillating college baseball career.

The stories about various Major League Baseball ballgames are easier to document and verify. I used baseball.reference.com, which provides excellent play-by-play accounts of all playoff and World Series games that were played in my lifetime, to double-check my memory as to these games. Baseball.reference.com saved me from several errors. In my mind, for instance, I saw Craig Counsell, rather than Jay Bell, run home from third base with the winning run in Game Seven of the 2001 World Series between the New York Yankees and Arizona Diamondbacks.

About the Author

Kevin Thomas Mulhearn was born and raised in Brooklyn, New York. He graduated from Poly Prep High School (Brooklyn) in 1982, Muhlenberg College (Allentown, Pennsylvania) in 1986, and Villanova University School of Law (Villanova, Pennsylvania) in 1990.

Kevin has practiced law (mostly in New York State) for twenty-five years. For the past ten years, his practice has specialized in complex, multi-party civil litigation (including several high-profile school sex abuse cover-up cases).

He is the Founder and Publisher of Hard Nock Press, LLC (established in 2013), an independent press committed to providing a voice for individuals not afraid to challenge the status quo or "conventional wisdom."

Kevin has published numerous articles in the *New York Daily News* and other newspapers. His first book, *An Antidote for Injustice*, was published by Hard Nock Press in 2013.

Kevin lives with his family in Orangeburg, New York. He coaches Little League baseball and youth soccer.

Other Books Published by Hard Nock Press

An Antidote for Injustice: A New Paradigm for Winning "Old" Sexual Abuse Cases Against Complicit Private Schools (2013),
by Kevin Thomas Mulhearn

Grand Delusions: A Story of Mental Illness, Hope and Love (2015),
by Dennis John Mulhearn

You may visit our website at www.HardNockPress.com